Cambridge Elements

Elements in the History and Politics of Fascism
edited by
Federico Finchelstein
The New School for Social Research
António Costa Pinto
University of Lisbon

THE FIVE AGES OF ANTIFASCISM

Joseph Fronczak
Princeton University

CAMBRIDGE UNIVERSITY PRESS

Shaftesbury Road, Cambridge CB2 8EA, United Kingdom

One Liberty Plaza, 20th Floor, New York, NY 10006, USA

477 Williamstown Road, Port Melbourne, VIC 3207, Australia

314–321, 3rd Floor, Plot 3, Splendor Forum, Jasola District Centre, New Delhi – 110025, India

103 Penang Road, #05–06/07, Visioncrest Commercial, Singapore 238467

Cambridge University Press is part of Cambridge University Press & Assessment, a department of the University of Cambridge.

We share the University's mission to contribute to society through the pursuit of education, learning and research at the highest international levels of excellence.

www.cambridge.org
Information on this title: www.cambridge.org/9781009619653

DOI: 10.1017/9781009619646

© Joseph Fronczak 2026

This publication is in copyright. Subject to statutory exception and to the provisions of relevant collective licensing agreements, no reproduction of any part may take place without the written permission of Cambridge University Press & Assessment.

When citing this work, please include a reference to the DOI 10.1017/9781009619646

First published 2026

A catalogue record for this publication is available from the British Library

A Cataloging-in-Publication data record for this Element is available from the Library of Congress

ISBN 978-1-009-61962-2 Hardback
ISBN 978-1-009-61965-3 Paperback
ISSN 2977-0416 (online)
ISSN 2977-0408 (print)

Cambridge University Press & Assessment has no responsibility for the persistence or accuracy of URLs for external or third-party internet websites referred to in this publication and does not guarantee that any content on such websites is, or will remain, accurate or appropriate.

For EU product safety concerns, contact us at Calle de José Abascal, 56, 1°, 28003 Madrid, Spain, or email eugpsr@cambridge.org

The Five Ages of Antifascism

Elements in the History and Politics of Fascism

DOI: 10.1017/9781009619646
First published online: February 2026

Joseph Fronczak
Princeton University
Author for correspondence: Joseph Fronczak, jmf3@princeton.edu

Abstract: A global history of antifascism from its inception to our own times. Its inspiration, and subject of critique, though, is a work of fascist history, Robert O. Paxton's classic essay *The Five Stages of Fascism*. Paxton influentially studied fascism by comparing national case studies and proposing a cycle of five developmental stages through which each national fascism might progress. In this Element, the historian Joseph Fronczak counters Paxton's method of stages with one of ages: Instead of organizing antifascism into national case studies going through stages, he organizes antifascism's global history into five ages, stressing the transnational causes and solidarities that pushed global antifascism to take form and shift shape over time. A further aim of this Element is to pose this history of antifascism as a counterhistory of fascism, a sort of epistemological experiment for rethinking fascism's history through a formulation of antifascism's history.

Keywords: antifascism, fascism, historiography, historical methodology, global history, transnational history, counterhistory, political ideas

© Joseph Fronczak 2026

ISBNs: 9781009619622 (HB), 9781009619653 (PB), 9781009619646 (OC)
ISSNs: 2977-0416 (online), 2977-0408 (print)

Contents

Introduction: Fascist and Antifascist Histories in Stages and Ages — 1

1 The Age of the Original Antifascisti (and Antifa), 1921–1932 — 13

2 The Golden Age of Antifascist Solidarity, 1933–1938 — 25

3 Resistance in an Age of Genocide, 1939–1967 — 39

4 The Age of Freedom Antifascism, 1968–1984 — 53

5 The Antifa Age, since 1985 — 65

Conclusion: Staging and Aging Antifascist and Fascist Histories — 78

Bibliography — 82

Introduction: Fascist and Antifascist Histories in Stages and Ages

Although what follows is a history of antifascism, the inspiration for writing it was a classic essay on the history of fascism. That essay was written at the end of the twentieth century by the much-venerated scholar Robert O. Paxton, based on a paper that he had given at the École des hautes études en sciences sociales in Paris in 1994. Paxton's essay, titled "The Five Stages of Fascism," appeared in print in the *Journal of Modern History* in 1998. Since then, it has been reprinted elsewhere and was also the basis for Paxton's 2004 book-length study, *The Anatomy of Fascism*, which has become a classic in its own right in the historiography of fascism. "The Five Stages of Fascism" has been broadly celebrated and widely cited, though the essay's greater impact is not of the sort that can be measured neatly by citational statistics but rather is of the sort that needs to be inferred from reading through the historiography with an eye toward its shifts and pivots. Evidence of the essay's historiographical impact, some of it obvious and some of it subtle, is imprinted onto a good portion of the scholarly literature produced since the publication of "The Five Stages of Fascism." It is there in the structures of argumentation, in the authorial vocabularies, in the givens of logic and points of reference, and in the methodological strategies that came to typify much of the literature. Paxton's emphasis on political practice; his phenomenological insistence on studying fascism "in motion"; his particularly disciplined, yet distinctly idiosyncratic, method of comparison; his embrace of explicit functionalism in defining fascism; his imaginative and open-ended articulation of what he calls fascism's "mobilizing passions" – all of these very Paxtonian wonts and techniques have soaked their way into the field well beyond the specific points in the texts where his work is cited.

What I offer in this work is an act of critical homage. Both the homage and the critique are sincere, and both are purposeful. Paxton's is a wonderful essay to think with, and, as with a good many great works, the thinking it invites eventually lends itself to considerable opposition.

In this case, the opposition hinges on those "stages" in Paxton's title. As I'll explain, Paxton's move to break the history of fascism into stages of development relates, for him, to one of his essay's two "principal methodological proposals" for studying fascism.[1] The crux of Paxton's decision to conceptualize distinct "stages of fascism" is that doing so

---

[1] Robert O. Paxton, "The Five Stages of Fascism," *Journal of Modern History* 70, no. 1 (Mar. 1998), 21.

helps him pivot to a specific set of procedures he uses for conducting comparative history. And for Paxton comparative history is the key to a more sophisticated and historically richer understanding of fascism as a whole.

The work you're reading, however, is not an attempt to understand fascism in the whole, but rather antifascism in the whole. At least, that is so in the most immediate, or most obvious, sense of the work's aims. Ultimately, though, my intent is to draw together the two histories so as to suggest that each is exceptionally revealing of the other: Fundamental to the study of fascism's history is the study of antifascism's; fundamental to the study of antifascism's history is the study of fascism's. From such a line of argument, it might quickly follow that one of the more urgent reasons to study antifascism is that doing so draws out into plain view certain qualities of fascism, including qualities generally obscured from the eye of the scholar who studies fascism head-on. One of the main propositions that prompted me to write this work is my contention that these qualities of fascism – the ones that appear at the fore when one approaches fascist history *through* antifascist history – are the very ones most in need of recognition and confrontation in today's world.

Though Paxton has paid very little attention to antifascist politics in his studies of fascism, my argument stressing the historical entanglement of the two is, all the same, indebted to one of his main methodological arguments, an argument he presents in "The Five Stages of Fascism" in the form of a plea to scholars and students of fascism to study their subject "contextually." Paxton makes this plea to study fascism contextually after charging that previous scholars of fascism had failed to do so. The charge relates to Paxton's broader critique of fascism's historiography as it stood at the twentieth century's end: In his essay, he faults scholars of fascism for two widespread "errors of approach," to use his phrase. Based on what Paxton has to say about these errors, though, it would be more to the point to think of them as errors of conception, or even preconception, rather than as ones of approach per se. This is so because the two errors take place, in Paxton's telling, in the offending scholars' very starting premises, prior to any authorial act of textual argumentation, prior to any actual analytical movement – that is, prior to any *approach* – toward their texts' subjects. The errors have already happened, rather, in that nebulous zone of assumption and intuition from whence scholars might begin to piece together and launch their explicit arguments. The two errors are (1) the conception (or preconception) of fascism as if it were static and (2) the conception (or preconception) of fascism in isolation from its surroundings (or even as if it were an aberration *from* its surroundings, essentially atypical, or anomalous, inconsistent with the larger political order, even freakish).[2] Against the first error, the (pre)conception of stasis, Paxton proposes his framework of "stages," to which I'll come; against the second, the (pre)conception of isolation, he proposes a heavy dose of context.

Concerning context: For Paxton, to study fascism in isolation is to miss something elemental to its formation and potency. The crucial point, he stresses, is that any instantiation of fascism "is ensnared in a web of reciprocal influences with allies or rivals in its country's civil society." Consider two elements of this claim. First: Paxton's idea of context – his "web of reciprocal influences" – concerns fascists' interaction with their surroundings rather than the surroundings themselves. The "reciprocal" is key. By "context," Paxton isn't after the more vernacular meaning of the word – those surroundings themselves, or the background, environment, or setting. And he isn't after the typical Marxist implication – structure, or material base. (Paxton's explanation of and for fascism is always radically political; he treats the Marxist historiography of fascism with polite skepticism; he challenges it by emphasizing fascism's cross-class appeal and by generally minimizing capital's role; speaking more generally, one could say that in method, interpretative perspective, and scholarly temperament Paxton personifies liberal historiography.) Rather, Paxton's meaning of "context" is more etymological: he means "context" to signify the work of weaving something together, as if the making of fascism were the making of a textile (con- + texere). Then, the second point: The web of reciprocal influences that Paxton is stressing with his plea to study fascism contextually – so as to see the weaving together of the thing – is of a very particular sort. Aside from the one reference to "rivals" that I quoted earlier, Paxton unpacks his notion of studying fascism contextually by focusing solely on acts of conscious collaboration among fascists and their enablers – generally speaking, the "conservative elites" who have "opened the gates" of power to fascists.[3] In *The Anatomy of Fascism*, where Paxton has more room to explain, he details what for him are the two classic examples of conservative complicity with fascism: The invitation to govern that the Italian king Vittorio Emanuele III extended to Benito Mussolini

---

[2] Paxton, "Five Stages of Fascism," 9–10.
[3] Paxton, "Five Stages of Fascism," 10, 18.

and the similar accommodation that the German chancellor Franz von Papen afforded to Adolf Hitler.[4] As classic examples, these work well. What's more striking, and more consequential to Paxton's argument, though, is that he uses the discussion of conservatives' complicity as his analytical frame bounding his view of fascism's context. That is: studying fascism contextually, in Paxton's analysis, exclusively means studying the collaboration of fascists and conservatives. The collaboration encompasses the context.

But it's not much of a stretch to extend Paxton's basic insight – concerning the value of studying fascism contextually – well beyond where he takes this insight himself, in practice. Surely fascism's foes have shaped its history as well, no? To assume otherwise, or to leave the question of influence as Paxton leaves it, circumscribed by instances of explicit alliance and conscious collaboration, is to interpret influence as a rather straightforward, almost arithmetic condition of precalculated intentionality. (Paxton's intentionalist rendering of fascism's making is a good example of the ways his analysis fits so squarely within liberal historiography: Free agents compacting consciously to advance shared, albeit limited, interests and aims, their ideas given new form and their thinking given new shape by the exchange.) We choose our allies; we choose our influences. A denser reading of context – as a much more gnarled web of causative forces and dialectical influences, its tangles messier, intractable and inscrutable, with many of even the greatest influences strictly unchosen and absorbed only half- or entirely unconsciously – would prod its reader to embed fascism within a much trickier, eerier, more chaotic, and uncannier political domain, one marked by ideological strife, anxiety and confusion, force, fear, and illusion. Such a reading of context works well enough not only for making sense of fascism but also as a general rule for making sense of all the modern world's politics. Liberalism, say, is surely shaped by the conservatism with which it contends; anticommunism is surely shaped by the communism which it condemns. That said, though, well beyond any such general rule, the point applies with special force to fascism.

This is so for two primary reasons.

First and foremost: Fascism stands out among modernity's major ideological forms – the "great 'isms,'" Paxton calls them – for its practitioners' dramatic, meaning-making performances of violence and for their

---

[4] Robert O. Paxton, *The Anatomy of Fascism* (New York: Knopf, 2004), 96–101.

intense sacralization of violence.[5] To be sure, practitioners of modernity's other leading isms have deployed violence instrumentally (as have fascists). But – unlike the others – fascists have also put faith in violence as a sublime and transcendent metaphysical experience, a flight into expanded consciousness both transformative and revelatory in nature. Fascists have leaped into the enactment of violence as if to make of it an escape from morality into a volatile freedom beyond, as if to make of it a surrender to brute force's mercurial and ungovernable powers. (In this way, violence has served fascists as a rite through which to shed the very liberal consciousness of intentionality, rationality, and free agency that Paxton draws upon for his notion of context as freely chosen collaboration.) In short, fascism is made, most emphatically, not in its consensual acts of tactical alliance and transactional collaboration with conservatives but rather in the singular acts of violence that its adherents visit upon their foes and victims.[6]

The second reason is closely related to this valorization of violence, and it constitutes another of fascism's core values: hatred. That is, fascism also stands out among modernity's great isms for its practitioners' uninhibited, truth-corroding effusions of hatred and for the radical trust that they have put in hatred to unlock entire realms of arcane counter-truths and forms of power hidden away from normal political life. To be sure, practitioners of modernity's other great isms have acted on hatred and have disseminated it in myriad forms. But – unlike those others – fascists have also taken hatred itself as a code. This is so in a double sense. For fascists, hatred has worked as a code in that it has imposed on them an assortment of expectations and principles of conduct – it's *been* their code – and, more to my point, hatred also has worked as a code for fascists in that it has functioned for them as a sort of cryptographical key, letting them encode and decode their experiences according to a distinctly fascist script. Regarding the encoding: Among each other, fascists have worked out and drawn on specific and elaborate discourses of hatred to the point that they could be said to be speaking in code. A skillfully turned expression of hatred affirms fascist belonging and tightens its bonds. To express with dexterity any of the well-established fascist hatreds verifies one's exclusive belonging, it verifies one's fascism, like the adroit execution of a secret handshake. This is because it takes dedication to iron out the particularities woven through

---

[5] Paxton, "Five Stages of Fascism," 4.
[6] On fascism and violence, see Federico Finchelstein, *From Fascism to Populism in History* (Oakland: University of California Press, 2017), 73–81.

fascism's language of hatred, it takes dedication to speak the language fluently – to learn the code. Regarding the decoding: Out in the world, fascists rely on hatred to function as a sort of algorithm for deciphering the complex or otherwise confounding. An elaborately calculated hatred can descramble social life's information overload into a simple fascist plaintext. Again, for those who possess the code, it both encrypts and decrypts.

In sum, regarding the larger point of putting fascism in its proper context, beyond Paxton's frame of intentional collaboration: Whatever relation the theoretical friend–enemy distinction may have to fascist history, it is fascism's relationship to its enemies, and not to its friends, that has been the decisive, and the distinctive, force setting fascism apart.

Yet, set fascism apart as it may, this dynamic all the same obviously has implications for antifascism's history. Think of antifascism as critical context to the text of fascism; think of fascism as critical context to the text of antifascism. It's true that antifascism has meant, to those who have practiced it, more than the act of opposing fascism, but it's also true that the act of opposing fascism has been antifascists' main work – often to the point of obsession. More than most isms, antifascism has taken shape and been given content by the imperatives of its ongoing struggle against its primary adversary. Again, fundamental to the study of fascism's history is the study of antifascism's; fundamental to the study of antifascism's history is the study of fascism's. In the body of this essay, I sketch an outline of antifascism's history that might lend itself to a reworking of fascism's history, a reworking more attentive to the question of what fascism has looked like, throughout its history, to its most direct enemies (and most searching critics), throughout their history.

Those comments should suffice for introducing Paxton's idea of context. The plea to study fascism contextually, though, is not Paxton's main methodological proposal. His main methodological proposal relates to his use of stages to structure fascism's history. Tellingly, his proposal isn't a brief arguing for the use of stages in the study of fascism but, rather, a brief arguing for what he calls the "discrimination among stages." That is, Paxton begins the act of explicit argumentation at a point of logic already beyond any working out of his notion that fascism has, as he comments in passing, its own "cycle" of "successive stages." Because he bypasses the task of positing his notion in the form of a scholarly claim in need of justification, it remains throughout the text always a presupposition. Yet all the same it serves as the base for the two-part argument that Paxton does build: The argument that discriminating among stages is useful for comparison and that this is fortuitous because "comparison works revealingly with fascisms."[7]

Quoting a fellow historian, Paxton writes that "comparison is 'a way of thinking more than a method.'"[8] In Paxton's case, this is true. Elevated to a way of thinking, though, comparison comes at a considerable cost. This is in sharp contrast to comparison as a historical method: Historians typically rely on the method of comparison to draw out particulars about each of the subjects being compared and to prompt insights based on those particulars. For historians, acts of comparison are generally well worth the effort. But comparison as a way of thinking, to my mind, cramps the thinker's historical imagination in ways well worth fighting against and vanquishing. Paxton's model of "the five stages of fascism" is a case in point.

Consider one of the more telling aspects of Paxton's discussion of stages: that he depicts them as if they were object conditions, not as, say, heuristic metaphors he's leaning on to work through a larger idea. This aspect of his writing is related to his bypassing of the task of claim-making for his notion of stages. It's in the process of skipping that task that he implicitly poses the stages as objectively real. In his argument, the way this unfolds is that Paxton (a) argues for the value of comparisons; (b) qualifies that "one must compare what is comparable"; then (c) skips directly to the claim that, because one must compare what is comparable, "we must distinguish the different stages of fascism in time."[9] The asserted argument, the plea to distinguish, serves to smuggle past the reader's eye, and into the reader's mind, the notion that there really are such things as "stages of fascism." The asserted issue at hand is already the question of distinguishing among these stages that he has neglected to verify for the reader.

Regarding the work of distinguishing, Paxton notes that historians have long differentiated "between movements and regimes" and adds, "I believe we can usefully distinguish more stages than that." He explains, "I propose to isolate five of them." These five stages are (1) the "initial creation" of fascist movements; (2) their "rooting as parties"; (3) their acquisition of state power; (4) their exercise of state power; (5) "radicalization or entropy." This model for studying fascism, in short, is an outline of Paxton's interpretation of the historical trajectories taken by Mussolini-era Italian

---

[7] Paxton, "Five Stages of Fascism," 10, 21, 22.
[8] Paxton, "Five Stages of Fascism," 10.
[9] Paxton, "Five Stages of Fascism," 11.

Fascism and Hitler-era German Nazism. Paxton sees these two trajectories as parallel until the final stage, in which, Paxton assesses, Fascist Italy degraded into entropy, whereas "Nazi Germany alone experienced full radicalization."[10] For Paxton, then, it is axiomatic that Mussolini-era Italian Fascism and Hitler-era German Nazism were fascist – fascist movements, then fascist states. And it is axiomatic that they revealed fascism in its true and ideal form. Thus, for Paxton's model of comparison, they are the fixed points of reference, the constants against which all others are to be compared.

And so the logic of the model is a mix of idealism and empiricism. Paxton has an ideal of fascism in his head – and it is the empirical example enacted, in sum, by Mussolini's Italian Fascism and Hitler's German Nazism. The use of the "stagist" model, for Paxton, is to compare against these two prime examples any number of other instantiations of (potential) fascism. Through comparison of this sort, he seeks to "identify the principal factors in the varying success of specific cases, and even to isolate the constants." Paxton thinks in terms of specific and entirely separate historical instantiations of fascism. He sees these as radically self-contained and distinct – stressing the discrete and instantial character of his "specific cases," he refers to them as "fascisms," plural and separate. Thus, he writes of "early fascisms," "European fascisms," "first fascisms," "the first European fascisms," and the like.[11] Using his stagist model, Paxton asks what might account for the success or failure of a fascist movement to "root" itself as a mass party and thus develop to the second stage. He then proceeds similarly through the rest of the stages. According to Paxton's analysis, fascisms either successfully develop further or fail to through a sequence of check points – they either succeed in developing or they fail to develop. What does a successfully rooted fascist party do? It successfully acquires state power or it fails to do so. What does a fascism that has successfully acquired state power do? It either successfully exercises state power or fails to do so. What does a fascism that has successfully exercised state power do? It either radicalizes or degrades into entropy. The structure is rigid, even polemically reductivist.

It's worth asking, why would this be so? Paxton's historical model fits squarely within a broad mode of thought that became ascendant across the social sciences just as he received his academic training. This mode of thought became known as "modernization theory." More than a theory,

---

[10] Paxton, "Five Stages of Fascism," 11, 20.
[11] Paxton, "Five Stages of Fascism," 3, 10, 11, 12.

really, modernization functioned for Paxton's cohort of social scientists as a deep-seated, even reflexive ideology – more a general set of preconceptions or presuppositions than a conscious integration of claims, aims, and theories.[12] The engine of modernization theorizing was in the study of economics, but its logic became insinuated into every discipline of the social sciences. Its classic enunciation was that of Walt Rostow, the economist at the Massachusetts Institute of Technology (MIT) in Cambridge, in his 1960 book *The Stages of Economic Growth* (Paxton received his Ph.D. in 1963 from Harvard, hardly more than a mile up the road from MIT). Rostow posited that "all societies" lie "within one of five categories." They "develop" from one stage to the next (or fail to do so). All societies begin in the stage of "the traditional society." They then "develop" (or fail to do so) all the way to history's endpoint, stage five, "the age of high mass-consumption," exemplified by the United States since World War Two. As such, Rostow combined idealism and empiricism; he conceptualized societies as radically self-contained and distinct units; having conceptualized societies thus, he then categorized them into five stages; he did so by acts of comparison; for his acts of comparison, he relied on a prime example (the United States), his ideal drawn from history, against which to compare all others; his model's structure is rigid, even polemically reductivist.[13]

The developmentalist social thought that underpinned modernization theory also underpins Paxton's model of stages. The most striking – and, to my mind, most consequential – attribute of this developmentalist thought is its peculiar caging of time and space. Like Rostow's, Paxton's model seals each national society from its larger contemporary world, and it sets

---

[12] Michael E. Latham, *Modernization as Ideology: American Social Science and "Nation Building" in the Kennedy Era* (Chapel Hill: University of North Carolina Press, 2000).

[13] W. W. Rostow, *The Stages of Economic Growth: A Non-Communist Manifesto* (Cambridge: Cambridge University Press, 1960), 4–16. Walt Rostow understood himself, with his reductivism, to be countering a stage-based model of historical change formulated by Karl Marx. However, the historian and political theorist Gary Wilder argues that such a stadial (or "stagist," to borrow from Wilder's vocabulary) understanding of Marx's idea of history is mistaken. Wilder writes that "readers often interpret" Marx's references to past modes of production "as evidence of a stagist view of history. But I understand them, at least in Marx's late work, as attempts to identify a standpoint on the basis of which to claim that things really could be otherwise." For Wilder, readers often forget that Marx accentuated contradictions in historical forms of production; Marx did so, Wilder argues, to find emancipatory resources embedded within the contradictions. "Marx neither locates human emancipation in past social formations nor projects it to the end of a fixed set of developmental stages through which all societies must pass." Gary Wilder, *Concrete Utopianism: The Politics of Temporality and Solidarity* (New York: Fordham University Press, 2022), 167, 169.

each national society within its own internal time. For Rostow, there is a Year One in which the given society inhabits its "traditional" stage; it then develops toward what he calls economic "take-off" (or fails to do so), stage by stage. The place of the given society in a larger world-system of uneven markets, peculiar forces of dependency, unequal loan regimes, and with peripheral extraction zones and industrial production cores, and the like, doesn't factor. Likewise, the temporal context of world history – whether the given society was perhaps trying to achieve "take-off" in the midst of the First Industrial Revolution, or the Second, or the Age of New Imperialism, the Great Depression, or the Cold-War heyday of developmentalist economics itself – doesn't factor. Each instantiation develops within its own national container, its own internal time, unentangled in any goings-on of wider spaces and unembedded in any dynamics of denser temporalities.

Such containerization of space and time is fundamental to what I mean by "comparison as a way of thinking" and why it ought to be vanquished. Like Rostow, Paxton poses the nation as the inevitable unit of analysis. That is, not only does he treat each of his "fascisms" as a sealed-shut box, but he also seals each fascism precisely at a national border. In the text of Paxton's analysis, each fascism "fills" a nation's domain, and each is "fixed" firmly within the same. Thus, Paxton writes of "Portuguese fascism," "British fascism," "Spanish fascism," and the like, without problematizing them. As a result, the conceptual act of nationalizing each discrete fascism comes across as less an analytical choice and more a reflexive habit, an example of the tautology-generating mode of scholarship that Manu Goswami and other critical historians have labeled "methodological nationalism." Similarly to the way he spatially inscribes national fascisms, Paxton also depicts each of them as developing (or failing to develop) by a process unconnected to, and unaffected by, any context of fascism's larger history. Instead, each national example operates within its own encased chronos. Whether "Spanish fascism" were to enter Stage One in the world-historical context offered by, say, 1922, 1933, 1946, 1989, 2013 doesn't factor; regardless of the calendar year, the national fascism is initiating its own Year One of – to use Paxton's term – "the fascist cycle."[14]

Three further points of critique bear mention here. One: Eurocentrism. The Eurocentrism is hardwired into the model – you could call it a

---

[14] Paxton, "Five Stages of Fascism," 7, 17; Manu Goswami, *Producing India: From Colonial Economy to National Space* (Chicago: University of Chicago Press, 2004), 4–20.

methodological Eurocentrism – because Paxton's design is "hub and spoke," with his conceptualized compound of Italian Fascism and German Nazism working as the hub, the fascist ideal against which all other examples are to be compared. Two: What you might call Eurocentrism's obverse. In the essay's text, the axiomatic certainty of Italian fascism and German fascism works to license confident talk, more generally, of "European fascisms." The nation remains the basic analytical container unit, but by the essay's end Europe has come to seem the proper warehouse holding fascism's national containers. This has two effects. Not only is Europe presented uncritically as the proper home of fascism, but fascism is also presented uncritically as properly at home across Europe. Typically, Eurocentrism works this way: It not only privileges Europe but also flattens Europe, often making of it a uniform ontological object. Critiques of Eurocentrism ought to be carried out with care not to mirror the effect. Three: What you might call "interwar"-centrism. After all, Paxton's prime example of Italian Fascism and German Nazism doesn't incorporate, say, the Italian fascism of the Movimento Sociale Italiano, created in 1946, or the German Nazism of Deutsche Alternative, created in 1989. Paxton's Italian Fascism is strictly that of Mussolini's era; his German Nazism is strictly that of Hitler's. This means that not only is a certain pair of countries locked into place as the prime example against which all comparisons across space are to be made, a certain period of time is locked into place, as well, as the prime example against which all comparisons across time are to be made. For the prospects of conceptualizing fascism's history as a whole, the temporal wall Paxton builds around his fascist ideal is even more consequential than the spatial wall.

The metaphor of the wall signifies well the general problem of the stagist model, and one of the more urgent problems of "comparison as a way of thinking": The problem of "the present" in historical analogy. Paxton asks his readers to consider "the burning question of this moment: can fascism still exist today?" He answers by analogizing. His way of thought is to compare between the present and the past and to judge whether there are "new functional equivalents of fascism" in the present, or "new movements of an analogous type" – analogous to his ideal drawn from the past, that of Mussolini's and Hitler's fascisms.[15] The analytical problem with such analogizing is that it has preset into it a presupposition of a fundamental separateness: past/present. The act of analogy allows for – and even encourages attention to – similarity, resemblance, and correspondence.

---

[15] Paxton, "Five Stages of Fascism," 22.

But all the same, it begins from a preconception, or perhaps a conclusion fully cemented a priori, that there are (at least) two distinct things under discussion. That's the premise of comparison, and of any analogy to be drawn from it. In the text of Paxton's analysis, fascism is discursively walled within the past by his chosen structure of comparison, analogy, and equivalence. The things Paxton goes on to say regarding his analogy between past and present explicitly emphasize similarity between the two, but the implicit rules of analogy have already set up a hard barrier between them. The analogizing separates even as it pulls near. The result is a sense of the present overwhelmed by unending anxiety caused by an ever-present proximity to this phantasmic fascism of the past, which – ever-present proximity notwithstanding – remains always just behind the wall.

The five sections that comprise the body of this extended essay are meant to call forth a counterhistory to Paxton's "five stages of fascism." Not only do I turn to the antifascists, but also I try to turn Paxton's model of stages inside out. I do so to ask: What has fascism looked like to the antifascists throughout their entangled histories? The first thing to say is that it has not looked like any one thing. Antifascists have depicted various different sorts of fascism and various different sorts of antifascists have depicted fascism very differently from the ways that other antifascists have.

Regardless of that, though, two points of difference from Paxton's perspective stand out. First, antifascists have by and large understood fascism as a global politics. Second, antifascists have, somewhat as a rule, seen fascism as a presence in their present. And so as a counter to Paxton's model of fascist history in five stages and the closed developmentalist conception of history that his model represents, I've organized an antifascist history in five ages. My thought is that such a history is useful for drawing out these two points of difference. Time and time again, antifascists have created and shared with each other transnational causes and solidarities – the connections they've made, across national boundaries, have been fundamental to their politics. These causes and solidarities have been bounced around the world, far beyond Europe. And so taking antifascism out of national containers has a way of breaking down Eurocentric premises. For each of the five ages I propose here, I'll stress the ways – in the campaigns and the solidarities – that antifascists have built their politics as a fundamentally transnational project.[16] Part of their rationale, it should

---

[16] See Kasper Braskén, Nigel Copsey, and David J. Featherstone, eds., *Anti-Fascism in a Global Perspective: Transnational Networks, Exile Communities, and Radical Internationalism* (Abingdon: Routledge, 2021).

become clear, has been that the antifascism they make ought to take a global logic because fascism has taken one. Because antifascists have always reliably seen fascism at work in their present, antifascist praxis can work as a useful rejoinder to any claim consigning fascism to the past. More specifically, studying antifascists throughout their history is a way of learning to see the slow shift, as the ages accumulate, in what it has meant for fascism to be seen in the present, again and again, part of an ever-later present. History piles up. The layers of the past have been wedged into each new age press always in new configurations. I think the practice of working out antifascism's longer history, age by age, is useful for reckoning what a similarly structured history of fascism might show.

Yet it's worth stating plainly that this work's purpose is decidedly not to prompt you to adhere uncritically to an antifascist interpretation of fascism. My argument is not that you should simply see fascism as antifascists of this time or that would have you see it. Neither, though, is my argument that even the structure of this work ought to be applied directly to fascist history. If that were the case, I'd have written out a book in the form of "five ages of fascism." Rather, my aim in writing has been that the reader might think of this work as an epistemological experiment – a trial of sorts for figuring out what might come of an investigation into the insights into fascism that antifascists have drawn from their struggles against it. Read this work of counterhistory thus, and you might find yourself at its end to have gathered various useful intellectual resources for working out your own formulation of fascism's history, its place in the world, past and present, and its points of entry into the future as well.

1 The Age of the Original Antifascisti (and Antifa), 1921–1932

When Paxton situates fascism among modernity's great ideological forms, its great isms, he does so with a shrewdly historicizing sensibility. Boiled down, his argument has two parts. First, fascism is one of several imposing isms that have animated the political life of modernity, along with conservatism, liberalism, and socialism, which he labels the three "great 'isms' of nineteenth-century Europe." But, second, fascism is unlike these other three because of the difference of its own era of birth – not the nineteenth century, with its parliamentary politics of "learned debates" and "deference to educated leaders," but the twentieth century, with its unruly, impassioned, and participatory mass politics.[17] The world-historical context of fascism's time of birth marked its form. It's a

---

[17] Paxton, "Five Stages of Fascism," 4.

wonderful insight, and one that rather troubles Paxton's general framework of sealed developmental containers, each with its own internal time, in telling ways.

Like fascism, antifascism first took form amid the great ideological tempests of the twentieth century. Likewise, this marked its form. Paxton's insight into fascism applies just as readily to antifascism: Born in an age of mass politics, it was shaped at its beginning by an "ambiguous relationship between doctrine and action."[18] When people talking politics in Italy first started floating the notion that there was such a thing as antifascism ("antifascismo"), the talk very much did not have to do with the goings-on of politicians in parliament; the talk, rather, was almost always of political action in the piazza. The talk was of "antifascist violence" and "antifascist conspiracies" and "antifascist solidarity."[19] There are two dimensions to this: first, the early practitioners of antifascism were common people in the public square, not professional politicians in the parliamentary arena; second, the early references to antifascism were to material acts of mass politics, not to abstract expressions of political thought. Even when people's notions of antifascism began to incorporate a more emphatic sense of ideological content and doctrine, antifascism remained embedded within the praxis of mass politics. Typical of such notions was the opinion, expressed in the Italian Socialist Party's newspaper *Avanti!* in May 1922, that those "who make open professions of antifascism" weren't the politicians or the intellectuals but rather the rank-and-file war veterans who were joining militant organizations dedicated to opposing fascism.[20]

Aside from its markings of twentieth-century mass politics, consider three more points about the historical timing of antifascism's origin and early formation.

First, fashioned as it was in the years that followed the First World War, antifascism was a "late" addition to what was by then already a very crowded field of isms. This clearly had an effect on early antifascist practice and thought. Perhaps most decisively, it meant that antifascism came together as an ideological form that didn't demand exclusive commitment from its adherents. The early antifascists of Italy – "antifascisti" – were also anarchists, socialists, republicans, communists, and the like. Their antifascism, as it took form in their minds and practices, overlapped – and interwove – with their other ideological affinities. Such ideological

---

[18] Paxton, "Five Stages of Fascism," 4.
[19] "Le fortune del fascismo," *Stampa*, Jan. 30, 1921, p. 1; "Cronaca di Arezzo," *Avanti!* Sept. 25, 1921, p. 5; "Il fascismo e la lotta agraria in Puglia," *Avanti!* Feb. 12, 1921, p. 4.
[20] "L'ultima speculazione," *Avanti!* May 26, 1922, p. 1.

density wasn't exceptional of Italy but rather typical throughout the post-Great-War world. As antifascism was introduced into political discourse in more and more of the world in the interwar years, it did so always upon a landscape already thick with ideological diversity and commitment. This was a different ideological ecosystem from the one inhabited by isms in the nineteenth century.

Second, not only the twentieth century's mass politics marked the early makings of fascism and antifascism in ways that made them different from classical nineteenth-century isms, so too did the twentieth century's mass society and its mass culture. In particular, mass culture had intensified since the nineteenth century to transformative effect. The practice of newspaper reading in the nineteenth century, according to the influential argument of the scholar Benedict Anderson, had been pivotal in enhancing people's nationalist imaginations. Reading the daily news drawn from across a national territory, readers had imagined themselves and others around them into national communities.[21] In the interwar world, newspaper reading was a much more widespread practice; also, though, the institutional and technological infrastructure of the newspaper industry had been transformed. Foreign correspondents, telegraph networks, and international news agencies had radically transnationalized the daily news. Readers imagined themselves and others now into dramatically transnational political communities. Readers' sense of contemporaneity had expanded as well. The zone in which their present moment could be imagined to unfold became almost global in scope, and so, for example, the growths of fascism in Italy and in Germany were events of global politics in a new manner. Another reason for mass culture's intensified powers was that newspapers no longer monopolized people's engagement with the goings-on of their unfolding present – with "the news." Radio and newsreel cinema were also giving people ways to connect to world affairs; this had the effect of making isms more immediately accessible, more democratically accessible, and more participatory in their nature. Radio and newsreel also intensified the transnationalizing effect of the era's newspapers. (And yet, for all the new transnationalizing force of interwar mass culture, none of this outright replaced the nationalizing force of it that had been at work already in the nineteenth century; rather, it added countervailing force; but that's not all it did: Radio and newsreel also worked additively to intensify nationalist imaginations, even as they also

---

[21] Benedict Anderson, *Imagined Communities: Reflections on the Origin and Spread of Nationalism* (London: Verso, 1991).

provided the new transnationalizing force. Such contradictory dynamics help to explain the conundrum of fascism's simultaneous transnational transmissibility and ultranationalist passions.) This mass cultural revolution both reshaped the "classical" isms handed down from the nineteenth century and shaped the new isms from the moments of their origins.

Third, even though antifascism was first fashioned in the early 1920s, it was not right away fashioned in the ready-made form of a great, universal ism. Rather, it started out as a particularism of Italian popular politics. The same had been so of fascism, when it had first begun to cohere into a political form during and immediately after the First World War.[22] To make sense of antifascism's or fascism's place among modernity's great isms, you do well first to pay attention to the gradual nature of each form's making – beginning as a particularism, reimagined over time into a universal. By the time of antifascism's birth, Paxton's three "great 'isms' of nineteenth-century Europe" had all been worked into universals of global politics. Their utterance carried the implication that they were natural facts of life, objective omnipresences throughout the world's politics. This, of course, wasn't strictly true; it was, rather, simply the work of people's political imaginations. At the same time, though, the early imaginings of fascism and antifascism didn't pose them as universals; instead, they pocketed them in Italy, in a fashion akin to the ways people might discuss peronismo as a particularism of Argentina's political life or Trumpism as a particularism of the United States'. This also was, or is, imaginative work, and one of the main tasks of this section of the essay is to lay out a few ways that people's actions, over time, worked to prompt new rounds of reimagining fascism and antifascism as ideological forms with larger and larger habitats.

Throughout modernity, though, universals and particularisms have coexisted in people's political discourses, often causing considerable problems of logic for each other. A certain sort of friction is generated by rubbing together the particular and the universal. One helpful way of observing such friction is to look at the ways that writers writing in languages other than Italian handled the terms drawn from Italian-language political discourse. It's a mistake to assume that the Italian "fascismo" of the late 1910s was readily translated "into English" as "fascism" from the start. Likewise, "antifascismo" as "antifascism." Or "fascisti" and

---

[22] For early references to "fascismo," see, for example, "Notizie di Milano," *Avanti!* Dec. 11, 1916, p. 3; "Note alla seduta," *Avanti!* Nov. 24, 1918, p. 1; Francesco Ciccotti, "La dittatura della menzogna," *Stampa*, Aug. 27, 1919, p. 1.

"antifascisti" as "fascists" and "antifascists." Early on, there was mostly confusion. One reader of the *New York Times* wrote a letter to the editor in 1922 asking for some clarification on the meaning of "Fascisti" and other such labels. "The London Spectator speaks of the 'Fascismo movement,'" the reader wrote, "and a New York paper refers to 'the Bavarian brand of Fascismo.' 'Fascista' seems to be another adjectival form .... Another paper ... calls a certain man a 'Fascisto,' of which 'Fascisti' seems to be the plural." The curious letter writer pleaded: "For the benefit of your readers, please inform us whether the above words are the correct words to be added to the English vocabulary of world politics."[23] Political language was in this era, as ever, a riot of creative loanwords, grammatically suspect "mistranslations," and clumsy transliterations. In retrospect, thinking somewhat teleologically, one might see no problem with drawing from a 1921 passage written in Italian containing a reference to "antifascisti" and translating the word as "antifascists." But at the time things were hardly so clear. (Ostensibly) English-language sources were full of (ostensibly exclusively) Italian-language terms. Political discourse was something of a cosmopolitan translinguistic mash. And so because my aim here is to point to the labor involved in making antifascism into one of modernity's sweeping isms, I think it's useful to signal the linguistic openness of the era by writing, for now, hopefully not too awkwardly, of antifascisti (and fascisti), along with a few tactical references to antifascismo (and fascismo). The point, regardless, is to stress both the particular transnational openness of the age's politics and the difference of fascism's and antifascism's meanings at the time from what would come later.

That being so, what remains of this first section of the essay's body will relate a short history of antifascism's origins, with attention to its mass-political constitution, the ideological density it encountered from the start, and its entanglement within the transnational workings of mass culture. Throughout, the broader aim is to "unthink" nationally containerized ways of thinking – and other nationalist thoughtways – and to rethink the historical makings of modernity's most grandiose ideological forms, its "great 'isms.'"

The early expression of "antifascist solidarity" that I mentioned at one point earlier was that of the agrarian proletariat of Puglia in southern Italy, as documented by a correspondent in the city of Bari writing to *Avanti!* in February 1921. The March on Rome was still almost two years in the future; the fascist movement was in a state of sharp internal division;

---

[23] R. D. H., "As to the Fascisti." *New York Times*, Dec. 5, 1922, p. 18.

Mussolini was far from state power. The power the fascisti possessed, and exercised, in early 1921 was that of violence. The key organization was not the political party but the paramilitary squad. "Squadristi" waged campaigns of terror and brutality up and down Italy. They fought those who sought to collectivize the land or to organize labor. Ideologically, fascismo at the onset of 1921 was a mix of mystical and exclusionary nationalism, glorification of violence, and – increasingly – bourgeois class outrage at the revolutionism of the postwar Italian proletariat and its politics of socialism, anarchism, and communism.[24] In Puglia, working-class resistance against fascist violence hit its peak by February's end, when laborers waged a three-day general strike across the region.[25] It was a spectacular display of mass defiance and refusal. As reported in *Avanti!* during the strike: "The insurrection of the Pugliese proletariat against the methods of intimidation used by the fascisti has assumed a truly grandiose aspect."[26] Before the strike, the socialist Arturo Vella barnstormed Puglia, rallying the workers. The fascisti of Spinazzola, a commune in the Pugliese interior, had warned Vella not to come. When he did, he paraded past their headquarters – the local "fascio" – along with a crowd of 500 peasants. Such a display exemplified what the correspondent wrote of as the "total enthusiasm and full antifascist solidarity of the proletariat" in Puglia. And it was effective – when the peasants' parade passed the fascio, the fascisti present "did not let out a shout or whistle." The anger of the peasants was palpable, but they also held themselves back from any violent outburst – "ahead of the action," the correspondent explained, there had been talk meant to cultivate a consensus among the peasants to put their collective trust in both "the resistance and the calm of the strong." This early example of antifascist solidarity, then, showed antifascism to be a politics manifest in the direct action of a crowd, organized informally, rooted in the local struggle of the working class, and positioned at the razor's edge where violence and nonviolence meet. The solidarity was also, the correspondent noted, a politics dense with ideological diversity. The antifascist solidarity practiced, the correspondent wrote, was the collective labor of participants "of all schools: socialists, anarchists, communists, and syndicalists."[27]

---

[24] See Adrian Lyttelton, *The Seizure of Power: Fascism in Italy, 1919–1929*, third edition (London: Routledge, 2004), 42–76.
[25] Frank M. Snowden, *Violence and Great Estates in the South of Italy: Apulia, 1900–1922* (Cambridge: Cambridge University Press, 1986), 191.
[26] "La formidabile insurrezione della Puglia rossa contro la violenza fascista," *Avanti!* Feb. 26, 1921, p. 1.
[27] "Fascismo e la lotta agraria in Puglia," p. 4.

In short, then, the solidarity shown in Puglia in February 1921 was richly indicative of antifascist politics at its origin.

That the earliest outbursts of antifascism were largely the informal acts of crowds likely influenced the shaping of the Arditi del Popolo, a people's militia that historians have recognized as the first coherent antifascist movement in the world.[28] Though it was a formal organization, its emphasis was always on movement making, never on institution building. The Arditi del Popolo first marched in Rome on July 6, 1921; local labor groups had organized a rally to mark "Proletarian Day."

At the rally, the Arditi del Popolo was tasked with providing security from fascist attack. But the group's larger task wasn't simply instrumental; by amassing a people's antifascist army that dressed, marched, and sang with dramatically stylized performativity and a sense of aesthetic spectacle, the Arditi del Popolo sought literally to show the people how to fight fascism. The "Arditi" in the group's name drew on the legacy of elite military units from the Great War – "gli arditi" were "the daring ones." The Arditi del Popolo sought to take daring direct action; they were a paramilitary meant to defend the people against fascism, and to do so in a fashion that inspired the people to defend themselves. The "Popolo" marked the group as populist – "del Popolo" meaning "of the people." The organization was entirely cross-ideological, welcoming anarchists, socialists, communists, republicans, syndicalists, and the like. No one political party dominated – indeed, each of the left's two main parties was displeased to see a group that it didn't control suddenly gain prominence.

Against the parties' demands of almost exclusive loyalty, the Arditi del Popolo practiced a politics of unity – unity across both party lines and ideological ones. As their participation on Proletarian Day would suggest, they were grounded in the working class. They practiced and stressed solidarity, not only with each other and within the working class, in a generic way, but also specifically as a way of connecting the near and the far: for the Arditi del Popolo, solidarity was a practice of overcoming spatial disconnection. When the fascisti descended on Rome for a congress to found a national fascist party ("il Partito Nazionale Fascista") in November 1921, the Arditi del Popolo took part in organizing a citywide general strike. The fascisti came to Rome not only to organize their party but also to make a public show of dominance and

---

[28] Stanislao G. Pugliese, ed., *Fascism, Anti-Fascism, and the Resistance in Italy: 1919 to the Present* (Lanham: Rowman & Littlefield, 2004), 55; Mark Bray, *Antifa: The Anti-Fascist Handbook* (Brooklyn: Melville House, 2017), 13.

provocation. In response, mass resistance spilled out of the working-class neighborhoods. The Arditi del Popolo took part in the resistance, which was readily identified in the press as "antifascist." For example, after the death of two men challenging fascisti arriving by train, it was explained, with some understatement, in the liberal daily the *Stampa* that "it is not yet clear to which party they belonged but they seem to have been anti-fascisti." The report added, "Most of the injured are fascisti."[29] The general strikers themselves also identified their work as antifascist. A manifesto published during the strike declared: "Proletarians! The antifascist strike continues, solid and disciplined."[30]

The Arditi del Popolo and the other antifascisti with whom they collaborated did much to define the shape of early antifascism, but even in this formative period antifascism wasn't encased in Italy. In the early 1920s, locals in New York City were also working their way toward a politics of antifascism. The central figure in their efforts was Carlo Tresca, the dedicated labor organizer and longtime revolutionary who edited the *Martello*, an Italian-language New York newspaper. During the Great War, Tresca had protested both the war in general and Italy's intervention in particular. From across the Atlantic in the United States, he had taken note as Mussolini devolved into the notorious demagogue of "interventismo," as the cause to push Italy into war was called. After the war, Tresca remained a constant critic of Mussolini and gradually learned how to become an antifascist. In June 1920, before there was any specific talk of antifascism, the *Martello* warned its readers that, in Italy, "yesterday's interventisti are today's reactionaries," betraying the nation's proletariat and serving its bourgeoisie. Mussolini was the main protagonist of this betrayal, to the point that the paper referred to the whole bunch as "the Mussolinis" ("i Mussolini"). Regarding these Mussolinis, Tresca's paper exhorted its readers to "spit all our contempt in their faces." The *Martello* also challenged its readers to consider that there were more Mussolinis hidden among them right there in New York City. The paper recommended that its readers spit their contempt in the faces "of all the little Mussolinis of America, should they ever dare to raise their heads from the sludge of their stupor."[31] The following year, Tresca was condemning fascismo in Italy as a counterrevolutionary form and mocking the fascisti of Italy as cowards who talk a lot but then hide in the attic once

---

[29] "Un'altra giornata di conflitti con morti e feriti a Roma," *Stampa*, Nov. 11, 1921, p. 1.
[30] "Il Governo per l'ordine pubblico," *Stampa*, Nov. 12, 1921, p. 1.
[31] "Come parla il rinnegato Mussolini," *Martello*, June 15, 1920, p. 9.

a fight starts.[32] Later, but still before the March on Rome, Tresca started holding meetings near Union Square to further what he had started calling "our antifascist agitation."[33] Within a few months of the March on Rome, a contributor to the *Martello* from New Haven was sharing news of a recent episode in which antifascisti invaded a nearby fascist rally organized by a notorious "spiritual organizer of colonial fascism" in the New York area. At the rally, comrades had "arrived in droves, until the room was literally packed with antifascisti" determined to show, by their direct action, that they would not give in to the fascisti "prowling the colonies, trying to inject into them the poison of the Mussolinian gangs." This was, according to the *Martello*, "practical antifascism," the sort of political statement that had been made possible because the antifascisti invading the fascist rally had "done away with the usual academic phraseology" of politics and instead committed to "concerted action." They had been inspired to do so, the contributor stated, by the antifascisti of Brooklyn, who had recently likewise crashed local fascist rallies.[34]

The antifascisti of New York and its surroundings weren't alone in exemplifying the ways that antifascismo was hammered into form not only in Italy but also far from it. Scenes similar to that of New York played out in London and Buenos Aires. The earliest antifascisti in London were the radicals who gathered at the King Bomba, the produce shop in the middle of the city's Italian colony, run by the charismatic old anarchist Emidio Recchioni. In July 1922, the group began publishing the *Comento*, a magazine meant as a weapon of propaganda aimed at both the fascisti in Italy and those that the magazine's makers were encountering in London – fascisti such as Achille Bettini, a hotel worker who prowled the streets of Soho in blackshirt uniform and claimed to have been one of the original 100 fascisti of Milan. By the end of March the following year, the antifascisti of London were organizing public meetings.[35] By the end of May, antifascisti in Buenos Aires were taking the same course of action that the antifascisti of Brooklyn had taken: showing up at fascist rallies and directly challenging local fascisti. They did so at a local theater and also at an Italian mutual aid society in the city center – there the confrontation involved more than 200 people as well as gunfire.[36]

---

[32] Carlo Tresca, "Fascismo e Fascisti," *Martello*, Mar. 12, 1921, p. 1.
[33] "Contro il fascismo," *Martello*, Oct. 7, 1922, p. 3.
[34] "Antifascismo pratico," *Martello*, Mar. 31, 1923, p. 4.
[35] Joseph Fronczak, *Everything Is Possible: Antifascism and the Left in the Age of Fascism* (New Haven: Yale University Press, 2023), 87–88.
[36] Ronald C. Newton, "*Ducini, Prominenti, Antifascisti*: Italian Fascism and the Italo-Argentine Collectivity, 1922–1945," *Americas* 51, no. 1 (July 1994), 47.

All these antifascist movements stretched people's understandings of antifascism beyond Italy's borders. But they did so largely by marking antifascism as a politics enclosed within Italy and its diaspora, a politics of "greater Italy," practiced by Italian people wherever they were in the world. By contrast, in 1923 Communists in Germany, led by the legendary radical Clara Zetkin, worked to fashion an antifascist politics that could be practiced by the working people of any nation. Zetkin's efforts, though, were soon stymied by opposition within the bureaucracy of the Communist International.[37]

With Zetkin's efforts cut short, the work of pushing the form of antifascism beyond its early greater-Italian particularism fell to antifascism's first epic cause, that of the global movement to memorialize Giacomo Matteotti. Kidnapped in Rome and murdered by fascisti in June 1924, the socialist parliamentary deputy had been a charismatic and courageous antifascist orator. Antifascisti throughout the world mourned his death and held him up as the great martyr of their cause. Holding him up thus, they attracted countless sympathizers, including those who weren't Italian at all, to the cause.

Mass mourning became a source of mass mobilization.[38] Memorial gatherings swept in newcomers to antifascism in cities such as Geneva, Nice, Paris, London, Boston, New York, Philadelphia, Veracruz, Havana, Port-au-Prince, Buenos Aires, and São Paulo. Many of the events were fiery affairs. At the London meeting, held in Trafalgar Square, local fascisti showed up to taunt the mourners.[39] Over time, Matteotti's memory became a collective responsibility to defy fascism without fear, as Matteotti had done. He had spoken openly of fascist terrorism and brutality even when it had become clear he was a marked man. The impunity with which the fascisti had murdered him stirred expressions of indignation throughout the world. In a message published widely, Italian socialist dissidents wrote two years after his death that Matteotti had become a force greater in death than he had been in life. "He has become the imperishable symbol

---

[37] On Clara Zetkin's efforts, see Kasper Braskén, "Making Anti-Fascism Transnational: The Origins of Communist and Socialist Articulations of Resistance in Europe, 1923–1924," *Contemporary European History* 25, no. 4 (Nov. 2016): 573–596. On the bureaucratic opposition, see Fronczak, *Everything Is Possible*, 79–86.

[38] On the mobilizational possibilities of mourning, see Enzo Traverso, *Left-Wing Melancholia: Marxism, History, and Memory* (New York: Columbia University Press, 2016).

[39] Fronczak, *Everything Is Possible*, 96–97; "Riot in Philadelphia," *New York Times*, July 4, 1924, p. 6; Letizia Argenteri, *Tina Modotti: Between Art and Revolution* (New Haven: Yale University Press, 2003), 97.

of moral and human protest," they declared, adding that "the cult of the martyr dare not be confined to a mystic and inactive veneration. The fact of martyrdom must urge us on."[40]

Antifascists were urged on, as well, by the increase of fascism's power. Nowhere was this more in evidence than in Germany, where Adolf Hitler and the National Socialist movement he led drew clear inspiration from the fascisti of Italy. Likewise, the Nazis' enemies drew clear inspiration from antifascisti. The inspiration was made explicit in the naming of a paramilitaristic youth group put together in Berlin, within the German Communist Party, in July 1929.[41] The group was named the Antifaschistische Junge Garde ("Young Antifascist Guard"); it quickly drew the diminutive nickname "Antifa."[42] This group, which is little remembered today but which was the original Antifa, had many things in common with the Arditi del Popolo, including a commitment to organized and collective self-defense, a working-class constitution, a movement culture, a stylized sense of performativity and spectacle, the youthfulness of its members and the emphasis they put on youthful energy and strength, a physically courageous insistence on direct action, and a dramatic insistence on taking up antifascism as an essential cause. What made Antifa different from the Arditi del Popolo was Antifa's connection to a single party: Antifa was explicitly a guard of the German Communist Party, and it drew its members from within party circles. Relatedly, the youths of Antifa don't appear to have shown any of the ideological diversity that marked the Arditi del Popolo; they seem to have been, for all practical purposes, communists with faith in the project of the Soviet Union. One of their main tasks was to serve as a protective presence at communist demonstrations. Typical of their public performances was what may have been their premiere, at the August 1, 1929, antiwar rally in the Lustgarten, a park in central Berlin popular for political demonstrations. One witness described Antifa's members as uniformed "in yellow, green and black shirts with khaki trousers."[43] A banner promised "proletarian self-defense." The slogans of the day included, "War on imperialist war!" and "The only just war is civil war!" and the songs sung included "The Internationale."[44] With time, Antifa settled on using blue-shirt uniforms, and it became popularly understood that the shirts were meant to signify that Antifa

---

[40] "In Memory of Matteotti," *Nation* (June 2, 1926), 618–619.
[41] "Antifaschistische Junge Garde in Berlin gegründet," *Rote Fahne*, July 21, 1929, p. 12.
[42] "Der Eid der 'Antifa,'" *Berliner Börsen-Zeitung*, Nov. 19, 1930, p. 3.
[43] "Berlin Permits Demonstration," *New York Times*, Aug. 2, 1929, p. 5.
[44] "Der einzig gerechte Krieg ist der Bürgerkrieg," *Berliner Börsen-Zeitung*, Aug. 2, 1929, p. 3.

was a counter to the Nazi brownshirts. Weimar authorities, though, banned both the uniform and the organization. One youth arrested at an antiwar demonstration in 1930 for wearing a blue shirt – underneath a white shirt – pleaded that the only shirts he owned were one brown and one blue shirt (leaving unaddressed the white shirt he was wearing over the blue).[45] Antifa's ethos was militant – its members understood it as a "fighting organization" – and defiant of authority.[46] The "proletarian self-defense" that Antifa's members preached meant, among other things, a refusal to rely on the police for protection. One evocative description of the organization's reason for being was that its members were to show up at communist events "to hold up the proletarian fist in the face of state authorities!"[47]

The organization that the German Communist Party set up in 1932 to replace the Antifaschistische Junge Garde after the authorities banned it was Antifaschistische Aktion ("Antifascist Action"). This organization also became known as Antifa for short, and it is today much better known in memory than is the original Antifa. In part, the second Antifa remains remembered for its famed emblem with two flags within a circle. This emblem has in recent decades become once more a touchstone of antifascist iconography. After antifascists in Berlin launched the magazine *Antifaschistisches Infoblatt* in 1987, they started including depictions of the icon in *Antifa-Info*, though they also recomposed the icon by putting one red flag and one black flag inside the circle to signify antifascist unity of communists and anarchists.[48] When Antifaschistische Aktion originated the emblem, both flags were red; they were to signify the antifascist commitment shared in common by both communists and socialists. In practice, though, the German Communist Party was uninterested in making common cause with the German Social Democratic Party. A lack of interparty unity and a lack of cross-ideological solidarity bedeviled antifascist politics in the last years of Weimar rule and no doubt played a part in bringing the first age of antifascist history to its end.

In the age that followed, antifascists made a rule of stressing the imperative of solidarity. The negative counterexample that inevitably came up was always that of German antifascism in the final days of democracy

---

[45] "Braunes Hemd – blaues Hemd," *Berlin Volks-Zeitung*, Oct. 22, 1930, p. 3.
[46] Eve Rosenhaft, *Beating the Fascists? The German Communists and Political Violence, 1929-1933* (Cambridge: Cambridge University Press, 1983), 155.
[47] "Sühne für die Altonaer Erwerbslosen-krawalle," *Altonaer Nachrichten*, Mar. 28, 1930, p. 5.
[48] Bray, *Antifa*, 54.

before the creation of the Third Reich. In the age to come, cross-ideological and densely transnational campaigns of solidarity would generate a mass politics of antifascist unity shared across a near-global stage. The age to come would be the golden age of antifascist solidarity.

During that next age, largely because of all the far-flung displays of solidarity and common cause, the concept of antifascism would be imaginatively reworked in public discourse into something much more grandiose and far-reaching than the particularism of Italian and diasporic political life that antifascismo had once been taken to be. The concept would be reworked into the sort of world-spanning, effortlessly generalizable modernity-defining ideological form that Paxton has in mind when he writes of "the great 'isms.'"

2 The Golden Age of Antifascist Solidarity, 1933–1938

Before antifascism became one of the world's great universalized isms, though, fascism did. The remaking of fascism from a particularism like peronismo or Trumpism into a universal like socialism or liberalism or conservatism isn't the sort of historical problem that's easy to analyze from within the confines of methodological nationalism. In a fundamental way, it's also the sort of problem that escapes "comparison as a way of thinking," in part because the comparative model presupposes plurality, and that presupposition gets in the way of seeing fascism in the whole – that is, as a totality, a thing itself, at work in the world of politics, rather than as only separate instantiations at work, separately, in their own national societies.

For Paxton, it's a historical problem that poses a conundrum. Much more clearly than some historians of fascism of his cohort, Paxton recognizes the problem – and recognizes that it is a historical problem. At the onset of his essay, he flags that the universal quality of fascism – the way that people have come to talk about it as a form of politics present throughout the world, unembedded in any one particular society – isn't a circumstance to be taken as a given but rather is indeed a historical problem in need of explanation. But his trust in comparison as a way of thinking works against him. It teaches him always to break apart fascism into discrete iterations – into the plurality of units needed for comparison. This is easy to see in the essay's constant references to fascism in the plural. Paxton writes of the "many early fascisms," "the first European fascisms," "past fascisms," as well as "today's neo- or protofascisms," and he writes too of "classifying fascisms" and qualities that are "latent in all fascisms."[49] His structure of comparison requires that fascism always be broken down into its parts; what people in history have meant by speaking of fascism in the whole is lost. Even though Paxton points out that he wants to figure out fascism in the whole, his comparison as a way of thinking repeatedly cuts him off – instead of looking for fascism in the whole, as he has set out to do, he ends up, in practice, looking for fascism in an ideal form – that is, he's looking at particular iterations to see whether any of them matches the ideal. For his notion of the fascist ideal, he relies on his conceptualized compound of Mussolini-era Italian Fascism and Hitler-era German Nazism. In his analysis, he ends up substituting this fascist ideal for any sense of fascism as a whole. In short, the basic prerequisite of comparison – to break into units – prompts Paxton to fall into his methodological nationalism – the notion that the nation is the proper unit of comparison – and it also prompts him to fall into the methodological Eurocentrism of relying on two European nations' "fascisms" as constituting his fascist ideal. Constant focus on the hub of his hub-and-spoke comparative model substitutes for any thought of the wheel as a whole.

By contrast, in this section of the essay I'll make the perhaps counter-intuitive case that the making of fascism into a universal took place because of political and intellectual work done outside of Europe, in the places left off the page in a Eurocentric analysis of fascism's history. And then I'll argue that the making of antifascism into a universal likewise took place, in a fundamental way, because of political and intellectual work done outside of Europe – not only because this happened in a way parallel to that of fascism's remaking into a universal but also because people throughout the world became antifascists to combat what they saw as the suddenly global menace of fascism.

That globality of menace is crucial for understanding antifascism's universal turn. It's a mistake to see antifascism's mid-1930s global boom as a direct response to the rise to power of Nazism in Germany. Nazism itself didn't directly provoke the era's global antifascism; in global politics, the more immediate effect of German Nazism's rise was that of example and inspiration for countless kindred movements eager to explore the possibilities of paramilitarism, exclusionary nationalism, political hatred, and public violence. Many of these movements expressed their fascism in their aesthetics – by marching in a hyper-modernist military style, by gesturing with straight-armed and open-palmed salutes, and by fashioning

---

[49] Paxton, "Five Ages of Fascism," 3, 15, 21, 22, 23.

and wearing paramilitary uniforms. Paxton is demonstrably dismissive of aesthetics – the "plumage" of a movement, he argues, is separate from "what may legitimately be considered fascist."[50] In the historical moment of the German brownshirts' rise to global notoriety, though, and in the context of the Italian blackshirts' similarly global notoriety, the multiplication of paramilitary movements insisting on color-definitive uniforms plainly demonstrated that these movements were communicating political content by displaying themselves in their paramilitary uniforms. It was a relatively global phenomenon. In the months after Hitler took power, greenshirts in Cairo marched; blackshirts in Lima did likewise, as did blackshirts in London; blueshirts organized in Canton and Shanghai, and likewise in Dublin; goldshirts marched in Mexico City; grayshirts were in Beirut and Damascus as well as Johannesburg and Cape Town; in Philadelphia and Chicago was a uniformed paramilitary organization known as the Khaki Shirts; in Minneapolis, silvershirts organized; black-robed terrorists in industrial Michigan were known as the Black Legion. Brownshirts in Newark held rallies with antisemitic oratory and swastika-marked banners (local Jewish boxer Nat Arno interrupted several of these rallies with stench bombs and organized an antifascist militia to confront Newark's Nazis).[51] Not only did each of these groups organize as a paramilitary, but each also advocated some form of exclusionary nationalism; each was violent and glorified violence; and each employed hatred purposefully as a mobilizational weapon.

One of the more forceful of such groups was the Ação Integralista Brasileira, active in São Paulo and Rio de Janeiro. The integralistas, as members were known, wore green paramilitary uniforms and thus became known also as greenshirts. They marched in the streets in military formation and provoked and intimidated with straight-armed salutes. Before founding the group and becoming its leader, Plínio Salgado had toured Italy and met Mussolini. Upon his return to Brazil, he had proclaimed that "the fascist conception of life will be the light of a new age." The greenshirts' chief intellectual, Gustavo Barroso, was a fierce antisemite who translated into Portuguese the notorious and fraudulent *Protocols of the Elders of Zion*. Barroso was a prolific writer and energetic ideologue, but he understood well the power of the green-shirt uniform to signify political ideas. As the historian Sandra McGee Deutsch puts it: "For Barroso the uniform was a public profession of the Integralista creed."

---

[50] Paxton, "Five Stages of Fascism," 3.
[51] Warren Grover, *Nazis in Newark* (New Brunswick: Transaction, 2003), 23–69.

Integralista organizers saw it as a means of mass organization; some of them recognized it as a nonspeech form of demagoguery.[52] In short, the integralistas exemplified the ways that fascism was a mass politics meant for mass culture. Their spectacular performance of fascism – street marches, outrageous statements of antisemitism, public violence, stylized salutes, and the wearing of readily decoded uniforms – was made for an age of newspapers and newsreels. They performed fascism not only for a local or national audience; they made transnational news, advertising not only themselves but also the sudden and spectacular globality of fascism. In grabbing such far-reaching attention, the integralistas wrote themselves into the ongoing history of fascism; more than that, though, they also reworked the nature of fascism. By practicing fascism *not* in Italy or Germany, *not* in Europe, they – and the grayshirts of South Africa or the silvershirts of the United States and so on – did the critical conceptual work to wear away the particularistic, Europe-specific texture of fascism.

The integralistas first marched in São Paulo on March 23, 1933. Not even two months had passed since the Third Reich had begun, and the day of the march was on the date that the Mussolini regime had set aside to commemorate fascism's anniversary. In response, various local groups of diverse ideologies took part in a meeting to organize an antifascist opposition in São Paulo. They met on June 11, 1933, in a union hall. The meeting had been organized as a commemorative affair of its own: it was nine years, almost to the day, since Matteotti's death, and his memory remained a potent mobilizational resource in São Paulo, most of all among the city's Italian community but also more generally among all socialists, communists, anarchists, and syndicalists. The Italian section of the Brazilian Socialist Party was named the Grupo Socialista Giacomo Matteotti. It was the Italian socialists that hosted the meeting, out of which took shape a committed local movement of antifascists. The participants named their movement the Frente Unica Antifascista ("Antifascist United Front") and they composed, and published, an antifascist manifesto to the people of Brazil.[53] The Frente Unica Antifascista included Italian émigrés, but it also included people without any personal connections to Italy. Just as the integralistas were the sort of actors behind the remaking of fascism,

---

[52] Plínio Salgado, "Como eu vi a Itália," *Hierarchia* (Mar. 1932), 205; Gustavo Barroso, *Os protocolos dos sábios de* Sião, third edition (1936; Porto Alegre: Revisão, 1989); Sandra McGee Deutsch, *Las Derechas: The Extreme Right in Argentina, Brazil, and Chile, 1890–1939* (Stanford: Stanford University Press, 1999), 258.

[53] "Manifesto da Frente Unica Anti-Fascista ao Povo do Brasil," *Homem Livre*, July 17, 1933, p. 6.

the antifascists of the Frente Unica Antifascista of São Paulo were the sort of actors who did the critical work to make antifascism into yet one more political universal – to make it into a form of politics that did *not* just belong in Europe. They acted in large part out of direct opposition to the integralistas – the understanding of fascism that São Paulo's antifascists had was centered on the local politics of the greenshirts; fascism was in no way a distant phenomenon exclusive to Europe. Likewise, the antifascism that they themselves began to practice. The June 11, 1933, meeting is as good of a marker as any for the advent of antifascism's second age, the age when antifascism outgrew its origins as a particularism and began to work in people's political imaginations as more of a universalized political form.

The integralistas and their adversaries in the Frente Unica Antifascista battled many times in the streets of São Paulo; their running street war culminated in a grand battle on October 7, 1934, in the Praça da Sé, the public square at the city's center. Antifascists ambushed a public performance of greenshirt theatrics in the square, and gunfire soon ricocheted through the surrounding streets. Thousands of integralistas and antifascists took part in the fighting. More than anything the integralistas had done before, the mass violence in and around the Praça da Sé made world news. In a way, the bloody spectacle functioned as a messy, ungoverned sort of joint political statement, made collectively among enemy combatants. When, in the days that followed, news of the "Battle of the Praça da Sé" was published in papers around the world, the stories inevitably communicated the message that both fascism and antifascism were political forms busy at work out in the world beyond Europe. Such statements by the deed effectively worked to strike down the older notions of fascism and antifascism as particularisms either of Italy alone or else of some broader and vaguely conceived but still Europe-specific realm. Such statements pushed people throughout the world – even those in Europe – to remake in their heads the politics of fascism and antifascism as universals, omnipresent political forms accessible to all.

The idea of antifa was also being reworked into a universal in 1934. This was due in part to the efforts of the Arab and Jewish social revolutionaries in Palestine who committed themselves to collaborating with each other to form a militant antifascist and anti-imperialist collectivity that they named Antifa. They stressed that local acts of solidarity, exchanged among Arab and Jewish comrades, could bring about liberation for all in Palestine and also could contribute to the global struggle against fascism. They portrayed fascism as a particularly bellicose and terroristic ideology of exclusionary nationalism; they argued that both Zionism and Arab nationalism had succumbed to its influence and further argued that the British Empire had intentionally propagated fascism on the ground in Palestine so as to divide its peoples and thus more easily rule over them. As explained in an Antifa pamphlet written in 1936, the imperial authorities had recently stood by passively during a "savage fascist surge," a "wave of terrorism," carried out by Zionist mobs, and then, "when Arab comrades of 'Antifa' rose up against the criminal activity of the fascists, they were the ones arrested and beaten by the police." The pamphlet concluded: "As usual, imperialism and fascism help each other and work hand in hand."[54]

Because of the efforts of Antifa of Palestine and contemporary groups such as the Antifa-Komiteen ("Antifa-Committee"), created in Copenhagen in early 1933, the concept of antifa began to take on a wider, more open meaning than that of a particularistic identity of the two German groups that had used the diminutive "Antifa" as their nickname in the past.[55] By 1934, those groups were both defunct; once the Nazis took power in 1933, the Third Reich quickly crushed Antifaschistische Aktion. By taking the name Antifa in 1934, the antifascists in Palestine likely meant to pay homage to the suppressed German group. In doing so, though, they didn't only honor the group's memory; they also implicitly provided new life to the group's name and claimed it as a marker for a form of politics that could be practiced beyond Germany, beyond Europe, out in the wider world. When Antifa of Palestine went about practicing that politics – militantly, creatively, courageously – the group effectively affirmed and contributed to a new and transformed meaning of the name-word, generalized by their very actions. And so in the same political moment that the concepts of fascism and antifascism were being reworked into universals, the likes of Antifa of Palestine ensured that the related concept of antifa would be as well.

The naming of Antifa of Palestine was an example of how freely and directly people can pull political forms to them and pull themselves toward a larger politics. The antifascists in Palestine who named their collectivity Antifa had no institutional connection to the earlier Antifas of Germany. Ideologically and organizationally, they were quite different. The earlier groups had been creations of the German Communist Party, affiliated with

---

[54] "Antifa" Palestine, *Les Troubles Sanglantes en Palestine 1936* (Brussels: Imprimerie Polyglotte, 1936), 3.

[55] On the Antifa-Komiteen, see the excellent Kasper Braskén, "'Make Scandinavia a Bulwark Against Fascism!' Hitler's Seizure of Power and the Transnational Anti-fascist Movement in the Nordic Countries," in *Anti-fascism in a Global Perspective*, eds. Braskén, Copsey, and Featherstone, 96–114.

the Communist International (Comintern) (as was the Antifa-Komiteen of Copenhagen). Antifa of Palestine was fiercely at odds with the Comintern-affiliated party active in Palestine.

If Antifa of Palestine pulled global politics onto their local terrain, other actors in the moment contributed to the globalizing of political categories by moving around, themselves, and carrying their politics with them. The fascist movement that took form among white colonial settlers in Kenya was typical. Josslyn Hay led the original organizing efforts.[56] Fascism made perfect sense to Hay. He had inherited a British noble title, but not before his family had sold the last of its ancestral lands. A product of Eton, he had undergone an apprenticeship in international diplomacy that had ended poorly. In 1924, still in his early twenties, he settled in the highlands of Kenya, where aristocratic white settlers had already established themselves as a force in colonial politics and economy. Hay quickly became the most notorious member of a notorious social set based at the Muthaiga Club outside Nairobi.[57] In early 1934, Hay spent time in Britain and fell in with Oswald Mosley, the leader of the British Union of Fascists, the paramilitarist party known popularly as the British blackshirts. The ideas and aesthetics of fascism appealed to Hay; fascism gave him a political framework within which to express his sense of himself as a man beyond conventional morality, a man animated by all-conquering action. He said he became a blackshirt because Mosley's movement "believes in action rather than talk." He spoke of "the obsolescence of the present form of government" in Britain and across the British Empire. Hay then returned to Nairobi to organize fascism there.[58] He argued that it was a mistake to conceptualize politics as if it were potted within a single nation. Against those who said that fascism had no place in Britain or in Kenya, he countered that he had never heard anyone discount socialism as "a foreign importation," even though it was "in fact far more foreign in its policy than Fascism." After all, he said, socialism was "for Internationalism and Fascism for imperialism." Instead of sealing off politics spatially, he situated it temporally. The age, he said, was that of fascism. Likewise, ages to come: Fascism was to be the "creed of the century."[59] In Kenya

---

[56] "Earl of Erroll As Blackshirt Delegate To Kenya," *Blackshirt*, June 29, 1934, p. 10.

[57] See Richard Davenport-Hines, "Hay, Josslyn Victor, twenty-second earl of Erroll," *Oxford Dictionary of National Biography* online (Oxford: Oxford University Press, 2004); Caroline Elkins, *Imperial Reckoning: The Untold Story of Britain's Gulag in Kenya* (New York: Henry Holt, 2005), 9–12.

[58] "Earl of Erroll As Blackshirt Delegate To Kenya," p. 10.

[59] Paul Stocker, *Lost Imperium: Far Right Visions of the British Empire, c. 1920–1980* (Abingdon: Routledge, 2021), 161.

he energetically organized fascist meetings among the white settlers of the Muthaiga Club and the large agricultural estates in the highlands, where the settlers sought to impose, as one of them at the time put it, "white settlement for all time." They named the homeland they had in mind and endeavored to secure the "White Highlands."[60] The idea of the White Highlands was the backbone of the settlers' politics in 1934. Hay and the other blackshirts in Kenya extended the idea and organized fascism in the colony using the slogan, "Make Kenya a White Man's Country."[61]

Within a year of its founding, the fascist project in Kenya ran into trouble and began to founder. In "The Five Stages of Fascism," Paxton writes of fascist movements "rooting" themselves at the second stage of fascism, "in which a fascist movement becomes a party capable of acting decisively on the political scene." He suggests that successful rooting "happens relatively rarely," because the proper rooting of fascism "depends on certain relatively precise conditions: the weakness of a liberal state … and political deadlock because the Right … refuses to accept a growing Left as a legitimate governing partner."[62] Such domestic conditions, though, weren't at all the problems facing fascists in Kenya as 1934 turned into 1935. Their main problem was abroad – in the global politics of the moment.

Benito Mussolini had decided to invade Ethiopia. That decision, according to the historian Paul Stocker, "changed everything … for fascism in Kenya." Blackshirts in Britain were enthused by the Mussolini regime's demonstration of imperialist bellicosity; blackshirts in Kenya were wary of the threat that an Italian fascist colony neighboring their own colony of Kenya would pose to their interests and ambitions.[63] Hay pivoted from building up a blackshirt movement in the colony to creating a new political organization to be called the Colonists' Vigilance Committee.[64] Conceived, as one sympathetic settler put it, as a force of "effective opposition" to liberal rule, and aiming instead to realize the settlers' agrarian vision of the White Highlands, the Colonists' Vigilance Committee also sought to establish, beyond the highlands, "a new, loyal, white Dominion" in East Africa.[65] Helpfully, in his analysis of

---

[60] "Kenya: The Settlers' Case," *Round* Table 26, issue 101 (Dec. 1935), 90.
[61] African XYZ, "Afro Readers Say," *Baltimore Afro-American*, Aug. 18, 1934, p. 4.
[62] Paxton, "Five Stages of Fascism," 12–13.
[63] Stocker, *Lost Imperium*, 162; also, George Padmore, *How Britain Rules Africa* (1936; New York: Negro University Press, 1969), 16.
[64] "Settlers Criticise Government," *Times of India*, Oct. 8, 1935, p. 5.
[65] "Kenya," 95, 97.

"the rooting stage," Paxton focuses on "fascism among farmers." He compares against the experiences of German and Italian agrarian fascism those of the French greenshirt movement, led by the pitchfork demagogue Henry Dorgères, which, like the blackshirt movement in Kenya, was organized in 1934. Paxton concludes that "second-stage" fascism consists of the movement's militants "being transformed into 'watchdogs' for the big planters." In Depression-era France, simply, "the French landowners did not need the *chemises vertes*" – the greenshirts. Instead, a strong and already repressive state and a stable power bloc of conservative landowners "left hardly any space in the French countryside for the rooting of a fascist parallel power."[66] Paxton may well be right about Depression-era rural France; the contemporary experience in Kenya, though, complicates the attempt to universalize dynamics at work in interwar Europe. Imperial rule, settler colonialism, the racial oppression of the majority, the acute hegemony of large-scale agrarian production particular to the Kenyan colony, and the organic political radicalism of the settler class (not to mention its vivid class consciousness and rapacity) – all these factors changed the calculus from that of contemporary France. All these factors weigh against the sort of analytical Eurocentrism that went hand in hand with the methodological nationalism of comparative history in its heyday.[67]

More to my point, though, is to consider Stocker's argument that the primary cause impeding fascism in the Kenya of the mid-1930s wasn't anything about the Kenyan political system or the state of conservatism in the national society; the primary cause was a turn of global politics, entirely beyond Kenyan borders: Mussolini's decision to invade Ethiopia. The political career of Josslyn Hay also serves to complicate Paxton's strict binary of fascist success/failure. Mussolini's imperial incursion just north of Kenya made political organizing in the name (and black-shirted uniform) of fascism an uphill haul, but the movement didn't so much fail as rather reconfigure: Hay fell right in with the radicalized white nationalists of the Colonists' Vigilance Committee. He hadn't fallen far.

Farther afield, Mussolini's warmongering against Ethiopia also worked to provoke the greatest antifascist mobilization the world had seen yet – a mobilization broader, more impassioned, and more consistently sustained even than the global movement of mourning for Matteotti had been.

---

[66] Paxton, "Five Stages of Fascism," 14.
[67] See Sebastian Conrad, *What Is Global History?* (Princeton: Princeton University Press, 2016), 3–16, 38–44.

The "Hands Off Ethiopia" movement of 1935 drew hundreds of thousands of new adherents to the politics of antifascism in cities around the world. People organized antiwar demonstrations in Rio de Janeiro, Buenos Aires, Kingston, Havana, Chicago, Detroit, Montréal, New York, London, Paris, Warsaw, Istanbul, Calcutta, Alexandria, Cairo, Accra, Lüderitz Bay, Johannesburg, Cape Town, and numerous other cities as well.[68] People began organizing protest against Mussolini's war plans in early 1935; by July and August there were demonstrations drawing in thousands of participants.

Some of the protests that took place in August 1935 – at a time when the League of Nations' and the various great powers' attempts to avert war were crumbling – were immense, teeming, participatory demonstrations of mass antifascist commitment. Consider four of the largest: in Harlem, Paris, London, and Chicago. These demonstrations showed well the new shape of antifascism. Like the meeting that launched the Frente Unica Antifascista in São Paulo in June 1933, these gatherings were the work of people who belonged to conflicting political parties (as well as those who belonged to no party at all) and who held diverse ideological beliefs; they were also the work of people with diverse racial and national identities.

Both in the European and the American demonstrations, Black antifascists took leading roles, both in organizing the demonstrations and in organizing the ideological content that spun out of them. An irony of the Hands Off Ethiopia protests of 1935 is that even though they directly targeted an aggression of Italian fascism they all the same worked to generalize and globalize people's conceptualizations of fascism far beyond fascist Italy. Typical of the antifascism fashioned by the participants of the Hands Off Ethiopia movement was the theorization of "colonial fascism" crafted by the Trinidadian anticolonialist and antifascist George Padmore. Amid his participation in the Hands Off Ethiopia protests, Padmore wrote a classic critique of British imperialism that was published the following year. He knew well about the ups and downs of Josslyn Hay's blackshirt organizing in Kenya; he nonetheless had a broader critique in mind when he wrote, "The conditions under which the Blacks live in Kenya can without exaggeration be described as Colonial Fascism."[69] The logics of antifascism – and the possibilities of solidarity it generated – gave Padmore and other anticolonial antifascists an invaluable resource for the totality

---

[68] See, for example, "International Actions in Support of Abyssinia," *Negro Worker* (Sept. 1935), 12–14.
[69] Padmore, *How Britain Rules Africa*, 16 (quotation), 129–130, 322–324.

of their political organizing and agitating. As one of antifascists who took part in the August 1935 demonstration in Paris, the Algerian anticolonialist Messali Hadj, explained: "We are antifascists, for peace, liberty and democracy ..., we are also anticolonialists, and we are for democratic liberties as part of a total emancipation."[70]

Padmore took part in Hands Off Ethiopia protest in both Paris and London in 1935, though he appears to have missed out on each city's largest demonstration, both of which occurred in August. The first mass demonstration that month, though, took place across the ocean in Harlem. On August 3, perhaps 20,000 people took part in a buoyant march through the neighborhood that ended in a street meeting near Colonial Park. The marchers sang and chanted, "Down with Mussolini!" Children held up signs stating, "Hands off Ethiopia."[71] The most vivid message of the march was communicated in its choreography: The demonstration began with two separate processions, one with Black marchers and the other with white marchers, many of them from Little Italy; the two processions then joined together and made one crowd; together they sang "We Shall Not Be Moved." The street meeting held in the Thirteenth Arrondissement of Paris on August 21 may have been even larger than Harlem's. Messali Hadj spoke and affirmed the solidarity of all Muslim people with the people of Ethiopia. Other speakers included other anticolonial antifascists: Ludovic Lacombe from Haiti, Paulette Nardal of Martinique, Paul Faure of Senegal, and Tiémoko Garan Kouyaté, an exceptionally brilliant antifascist organizer originally from French Sudan.

Four days later, antifascists held a mass meeting in Trafalgar Square in London. The small and effective group of organizers behind the Trafalgar Square meeting had named itself the International Friends of Ethiopia; its members were intellectuals such as C. L. R. James, Jomo Kenyatta (who at the time went by Johnstone Kenyatta), and Amy Ashwood Garvey. Someone from the British Union of Fascists (the organization to which Josslyn Hay belonged) handed out provocative and racist pamphlets among the crowd, but the provocation was handled without violence and the meeting went on. Indeed, the nonviolent quality of the meeting struck a newspaper writer in Chicago who read about it and referred to the calm in London as a point of contrast to the turmoil that broke out in Chicago when antifascists marched there just a few days after the Trafalgar

---

[70] Fronczak, *Everything Is Possible*, 171.
[71] Afro Correspondent, "'Respectable' Organizations Snub N.Y.'s Biggest Turn-out," *Baltimore Afro-American*, Aug. 10, 1935, p. 7.

Square meeting. The Chicago police were under orders to prevent the march from taking place, and they attempted to do so by carrying out mass arrests and by clubbing would-be marchers. Determined, though, the demonstrators still pulled off an unruly street parade, and participants afterward commented that they had drawn valuable lessons from the police repression. As was the case with the other mass protests of Hands Off Ethiopia, the Chicago parade had been the work of people with diverse political affiliations and ideological faiths. What had drawn them together was a shared intent to express solidarity with the people of Ethiopia; to do so, they had worked their way to solidarity with each other. The repression of the police was instructive in that it taught participants that the cause of Ethiopia and the cause of their own freedom of expression right there in Chicago were necessarily interlinked. Throughout the Hands Off Ethiopia demonstrations of 1935, protesters around the world learned similar lessons of local-and-global solidarity. In such ways, incident by incident, act by act, and experience by experience, was antifascism's golden age of solidarity made.

The most extensive lessons in world-spanning antifascist solidarity to be learned in the age were those taught by the Spanish Civil War. The Italian invasion of Ethiopia began in October 1935; resistance was fierce and widespread; Mussolini's forces, however, conducted chemical warfare, terrorism, and mass aerial bombardment; in May 1936 Italian forces marched on Addis Ababa and commenced a military occupation that soon became notorious for its brutality and atrocities.[72] Fascism was on the march: two months later, the Spanish Civil War began at garrisons in colonial Morocco, where generals in the Spanish army had conspired to overthrow the Spanish Republic by coup d'état. Overnight throughout Spain people mobilized to resist the military coup. The great communist orator Dolores Ibárruri famously took to the radio to issue her world-famous "¡No pasarán!" speech, calling on the Spanish people to defeat "the fascist military uprising." She asked all to follow the example of brave antifascists who were already taking up arms and taking as their battle cry, "Fascism shall not pass!"[73]

Not only the people of Spain answered the call. More than 40,000 people from the wider world went to Spain to fight fascism. Their efforts amounted to one of the great mass demonstrations of solidarity in human

---

[72] See Ian Campbell, *The Addis Ababa Massacre: Italy's National Shame* (Oxford: Oxford University Press, 2017).
[73] Dolores Ibárruri, *En la lucha: Palabras y hechos, 1936–1939* (Moscow: Editorial Progreso, 1968), 36–37.

history. They came from all over. Two brothers from Hanoi, Lucien and Peter Tchen, fought in Spain as soldiers in the International Brigades, the people's army organized by the Comintern for volunteers from abroad to take part in the war.[74] Two sisters from Haifa, Haya and Ruth Meites, set out from Palestine to join the cause in Spain; Ruth served as a nurse, and Haya ended up working in Paris to organize support there for Spanish antifascist forces. Among the fellow volunteers that Ruth Meites met along the way was Rachel Schwartzman, a Jewish teenager from Białystok determined to take part in the war effort.[75] Bernardo García Oquendo, from Lima, had been active before the war in the Aprista movement – the main bloc of popular antifascism in Peru – and had once even been condemned to death, suspected of taking part in an assassination plot; in Spain he fought in a militia of the Federación Anarquista Ibérica and then in the International Brigades; after the war he was held in a concentration camp across the border in France.[76] Felipe Torres was, to the historians who dug up his story, "the young Uruguayan who went off to the Spanish Civil War without telling his parents." He died in the Battle of the Ebro, shot through the heart, shortly after he had received a promotion for valor.[77] Chen Agen, a labor organizer from Shanghai who had drawn the ire of the Guomindang regime, was working in the galley of a French ship when he decided to take part in the fight against fascism in Spain.[78] Basilio Cueria, a middle-aged Afro-Cuban man from Havana who had played baseball in the Negro Leagues in the United States, fought in Spain as the captain of a machine gun company. "We can't let the Fascists put it over on us," he explained while on the front. "They'd put all the worst old prejudices back into force and probably even introduce some new ones, like Hitler and his Aryanism in Germany."[79] Over and over again, the antifascists who went to Spain to fight against fascism there made clear

---

[74] Hwei-Ru Tsou and Len Tsou, *Los brigadistas chinos en la guerra civil: La llamada de España (1936–1939)*, trans. Laureano Ramírez Bellerín (Madrid: Catarata, 2013), 271.

[75] Raanan Rein, "The Meites Sisters and the Spanish Civil War: Women's Support for Republican Spain from Within and Without," *Journal of Modern Jewish Studies* 22, no. 4 (2023), 503–521; David Diamant, *Combattants juifs dans l'armée républicaine espagnole* (Paris: Éditions Renouveau, 1979), 167, 169.

[76] Gerold Gino Baumann, *Los voluntarios latinoamericanos en la guerra civil Española* (Cuenca: Ediciones de la Universidad de Castilla-La Mancha, 2009), 167.

[77] Sergio Yanes Torrado, Carlos Marín Suárez, and María Cantabrana Carassou, *Papeles de plomo: Los voluntarios uruguayos en la Guerra Civil Española* (Montevideo: Banda Oriental, 2017), 22.

[78] Tsou and Tsou, *Brigadistas chinos en la guerra civil*, 202–203.

[79] Langston Hughes, "Harlem Ball Player Now Captain in Spain," *Baltimore Afro-American*, Feb. 12, 1938, p. 6.

that they did not see themselves as Spain's altruistic benefactors; over and over again, they explained that they acted out of solidarity with the people of Spain, that their own fates were tied together with those of Spain's people. The globality of fascist ambitions had pressed together humanity's political fates, and so antifascists had stitched together a collective response across the boundaries of their respective national societies. In historiographical terms, they had stepped out of case studies.

Their transnational bonding strengthened over time. Even as antifascists made the Spanish Civil War their great cause, many of them also became drawn to the cause of China, invaded by Japanese military forces in the second half of 1937. In September, imperial Japan heavily bombed Chinese cities. Given the context of the recent fascist bombing campaign in Spain (which included the notorious attack on Guernica carried out by Nazi Germany's Luftwaffe and Fascist Italy's Aviazione Legionaria), the devastation in cities such as Shanghai fueled the belief among antifascists far and wide in the globality of their struggle. For European antifascists, the war on China reversed the intercontinental dynamic of antifascist solidarity with Spain. Whereas the Spanish struggle drew the attention of the wider world's antifascists to Europe, the cause of China sparked the wider solidarity of Europe's antifascists. A British volunteer fighting in Spain drew the lines of connectivity plainly when he wrote in a letter home: "The struggle against Fascism here in Spain and the fight of the Chinese people against Japanese aggression in China are the most important points in the struggle against Fascism throughout the world."[80]

These points of antifascist struggle throughout the world didn't produce glorious victories. The Japanese Army marched into Nanjing, the Guomindang capital, in December 1937 and commenced a military occupation with a six-week-long massacre. By then, Fascist Italy already occupied Addis Ababa. Antifascist Madrid finally fell in March 1939; General Francisco Franco declared victory soon thereafter and worked to consolidate his dictatorial rule over Spain and its colonial domains. Still, the causes made to oppose fascism's advance drew together millions from around the world. Together, the participants shaped and practiced a shared transnational politics of antifascism. Together, they stood up against fascist regimes and also against the fascist movements that had multiplied worldwide. The conflict for antifascists, no matter where they

---

[80] Quoted in Tom Buchanan, "'Shanghai-Madrid Axis'? Comparing British Responses to the Conflicts in Spain and China, 1936–39," *Contemporary European History* 21, no. 4 (Nov. 2012), 542.

were, was taking place near and far, and its scale was both global and local. C. L. R. James, who had taken part in Hands Off Ethiopia in 1935, wrote, in 1937, "All the world must now fight against Hitler and Japan." James argued that even "the African enslaved by the Kenyan settler" and all others suffering immediate injustices of their own were all the same now "summoned to fight for the peace-loving democracies against war-making fascism."[81]

In sum, the fight was a world-spanning and epoch-defining conflict. The historian Eric Hobsbawm has written of the years leading up to the Second World War as defined by a "global confrontation" between fascism and antifascism, of which the Spanish Civil War was "the quintessential expression." The confrontation was, Hobsbawm argues, transnational in nature, global in scope, and yet all the same a civil war. This was "because the lines between the pro- and anti-fascist forces ran through each society."[82] Antifascist practices of solidarity drew together new comrades of diverse ideological beliefs, party affiliations, and national and racial identities; the practices of solidarity did so locally among multifarious sets of antifascists, and they did so over great distances, thus drawing together antifascists near and far. Like that of the confrontation, the scope of commitment was transnational in nature, operating both locally and globally, tying together the local and the global. The same could be said of the war to come.

3 Resistance in an Age of Genocide, 1939–1967

The great historian of the French Resistance Henri Michel argued that two different wars were waged in the years from 1939 to 1945: that of "the vast regular armies of the two sides" and also that of a "second war ... fought in the darkness of the underground." The scholar Donny Gluckstein has drawn on Michel's insight to claim that, though it had deep ideological stakes, the war of "vast regular armies" was ultimately a contest of empires, whereas the "second war," the war in "the darkness of the underground," was much more directly an ideological war. Gluckstein succeeds in teasing out many of the paradoxes of this underground ideological war by explaining it as its own double war: a war waged between

---

[81] Quoted in Tom Buchanan, "'The Dark Millions in the Colonies are Unavenged': Anti-Fascism and Anti-Imperialism in the 1930s," *Contemporary European History* 25, no. 4 (Nov. 2016), 664.

[82] Eric Hobsbawm, *The Age of Extremes: A History of the World, 1914–1991* (1994; New York: Vintage, 1996), 144, 156.

antifascism and fascism and also a war waged (not between empires but) between imperialism and anti-imperialism.[83]

It's an elegant framework for making sense of the Second World War. Ultimately, though, Gluckstein's greatest insights are not in the way he divides up the action into separate conceptual wars but rather in the instances when he interrogates the considerable friction caused by all the wars-within-the-war rubbing up against each other and complicating each other. All three dimensions of what might broadly be thought of as the Allied cause – the imperial war waged by the Allied Powers and the two dimensions (antifascist and anti-imperialist) of the ideological double war waged by popular resistance movements – incessantly got in each other's way, overlapped, clashed, reinforced each other in some ways, and confounded each other in others. The friction between the regular and the underground wars was felt most emphatically where their battleground was one, such as in Greece, where British Prime Minister Winston Churchill worked to thwart the antifascist resistance, even when doing so hampered the war effort against the Germans. Similarly, in India antifascist militants such as Jayaprakash Narayan drew the ire of the British colonial regime for waging war on fascism and imperialism at the same time. Narayan, though, insisted that this was one war only, and he invited the British to fight it with him. But he defied "the British fascists" who wished to fight Germany without fighting fascism. Narayan declared, "We work for the defeat both of Imperialism and Fascism by the common people of the world." The "fight for freedom" was, Narayan argued, both "anti-imperialist" and "therefore also anti-fascist for Imperialism is the parent of Fascism." If the Indian struggle for freedom hindered British war aims, that was a sign "that the basis of their war is false."[84] Likewise, Jawaharlal Nehru, also a committed antifascist, saw the entire war's proper aim as the defeat of both fascism (in the whole) and imperialism (in the whole) and the triumph "of true freedom everywhere." Nehru explained that even before the war began he'd come to see the causes of China, Palestine, Ethiopia, Spain, Central Europe, India, and elsewhere as "facets of one and the same world problem." Fascism and Nazism "had to go," imperialism "had to be completely liquidated."[85]

Narayan's and Nehru's arguments point to the problems of splitting the war into parts and leaving matters there. Anti-imperialist antifascists

---

[83] Donny Gluckstein, *A People's History of the Second World War: Resistance versus Empire* (London: Pluto, 2012), 7.
[84] Gluckstein, *People's History of the Second World War*, 47, 170–171.
[85] Kumar Goshal, "As An Indian Sees It," *Pittsburgh Courier*, Nov. 14, 1942, p. 7.

waged their war not only underneath the regular war of vast national armies; they also waged their own war *through* the other. Their practices worked to *convert* the imperialist war into the antifascist/anti-imperialist war, somewhat as the exiled communist revolutionary Leon Trotsky had urged at the war's onset. As Narayan observed in 1943, "War is a strange alchemist."[86] In July 1941, shortly after the German invasion of the Soviet Union that broke the two nations' collaborative pact and rescrambled the war, two Burmese advocates of national liberation, while in jail for giving speeches critical of British rule, wrote out the antifascist Insein Manifesto. The manifesto made the counterintuitive case for working closely with the British Empire to defeat Japanese fascism – and to end imperial rule. The two authors, Thakins Than Tun and Soe, arranged for the manifesto to be smuggled out of jail, and soon it was distributed in Burmese radical circles. As Thakin Soe argued, it would ultimately be "the contributions which we make to the success of the people's war against fascism" – and not anything "the British Imperialists" do – that "will decide the fate of the country." Thakins Than Tun and Soe sought to organize – and soon did take part in organizing – a popular antifascist resistance movement that allied with the British and yet also remained committed to becoming free of the British, all by waging the people's antifascist war – the Insein Manifesto's formal title was translated into English as "The Road to the Establishment of the United Front and to Launching People's War Against the Fascist Danger."[87] Two years later, the closest allies of Thakins Than Tun and Soe in "the Burmese antifascist resistance movement," as they called their cause, reinforced the message of the Insein Manifesto, stating that the movement believed that "the Independence and the Democratic affairs" of Burma "depend upon the complete destruction of the World Fascist System, which in the East is represented by the Japanese."[88]

Two months after the writing of the Insein Manifesto, a small group of antifascists in a very different place set out in a very different fashion

---

[86] Jayaprakash Narayan, "To All Fighters for Freedom," in *Jayaprakash Narayan: Essential Writings (1929–1979)*, ed. Bimal Prasad (Delhi: Konark, 2002), 84.

[87] Robert H. Taylor, "Burma in the Anti-Fascist War," in *Southeast Asia under Japanese Occupation*, ed. Alfred W. McCoy (New Haven: Yale University Southeast Asia Studies, 1980), 166; Jan Bečka, *The National Liberation Movement in Burma during the Japanese Occupation Period (1941–1945)* (Prague: Oriental Institute in Academia, 1983), 53, 299 n38; Tun Thwin, *The Impact of Political Thought on Burma's Struggle for Independence (1930–1948)* (Ann Arbor: Center for South and Southeast Asian Studies, 1989), 58–62; Martin Smith, *Burma: Insurgency and the Politics of Ethnicity* (London: Zed, 1991), 60–61, 439 n5.

[88] Robert H. Taylor, *Marxism and Resistance in Burma, 1942–1945: Thein Pe Myint's Wartime Traveler* (Athens: Ohio University Press, 1984), 198.

to aid the Allied war effort and, simultaneously, to convert the war. The group, based in Buenos Aires, Argentina, began by organizing a local knitting and sewing operation to make sweaters for Allied soldiers. The initial organizers decided on the name the Junta de la Victoria, or "Victory Board." It soon became a mass organization with thousands of members, all of them women. They thought deeply about the ramifications of their labors. As a group, they rigorously practiced internal democracy, and they also made clear that by clothing Allied soldiers they were aiding global democracy. Antifascist partisans living in a noncombatant, neutral country far from the front lines of the war, aiding the Allied war effort in the name of democracy, the members of the Junta de la Victoria were doing their part not just to win the war (for the Allies) but also to convert the Allies' international war of regular armies into the transnational antifascist people's war. Ultimately, they believed that the victory of the Allies – with that victory, thanks to efforts such as their own, rigorously converted into a victory of global democracy – would advance the struggle for national democracy in Argentina. In myriad subtle ways, the Junta de la Victoria worked to convert the war into more of an antifascist one.[89]

As impressive as the Argentinian group's efforts were, there's no doubt that the resistance movements themselves, in the occupied zones, were the engine of antifascist politics throughout the war. Though in memory they were inevitably drawn into separate national mythologies, in practice they worked in a necessarily transnational manner. Part of this, as the historian Olivier Wieviorka has stressed, had to do with the relative weakness of the resistance movements in any one national society. And so, unable to take on Nazi occupation forces alone, they had to rely on the Allies for help. But, ironically, the Allies were less interested in liberating any one nation and more interested in carrying out an elaborately coordinated continental, and global, strategy. The resistance movements' reliance on the Allies worked to draw together all resistance movements – and it also worked to draw together the war of regular armies and the war of the underground. The Allied governments and the resistance movements needed each other and thus incorporated each other into their plans. Even for emphatically patriotic and nationalistic resistance movements, this meant that at times they had to accept operating as part of a transnational campaign.[90]

---

[89] Sandra McGee Deutsch, *Gendering Antifascism: Women's Activism in Argentina and the World, 1918–1947* (Pittsburgh: University of Pittsburgh Press, 2023), 67–98.
[90] Olivier Wieviorka, *The Resistance in Western Europe, 1940–1945*, trans. Jane Marie Todd (New York: Columbia University Press, 2019).

Resistance in any one nation was also itself a diverse, polyglot affair. Movements were made of multinational volunteers, many of them refugees, fighting in whichever zone of action the war had found or thrown them. After the war, Charles de Gaulle had ample political incentive to depict French liberation as having been the triumph of a solid nation in resistance, but the wartime resistance in occupied France had included the work of many antifascists from abroad, including veterans of the Spanish Civil War. Joseph Epstein, a Jewish communist from Zamość, Poland, had fought in Spain twice; the first tour had ended in injury, the second in internment at the concentration camp in Gurs, France. After Epstein escaped from there, he joined the Polish Army but was outraged by the "fascist, racist ideology" of its officers. And so he joined the French Resistance as a member of the communist group known as the Francs-Tireurs et Partisans. Arrested and tortured, he, along with hundreds of other résistants, was executed at Mont-Valérien.[91]

The point to stress about organized resistance movements – aside from the heroism of those who took part in them – was their commitment to inter-ideological and interparty collaboration. In Yugoslavia groups such as the extraordinarily effective Antifašističko Vijeće Narodnog Oslobođenja Jugoslavije (AVNOJ; in English, the Antifascist Council of the People's Liberation of Yugoslavia), founded by Josip Tito, and the heroic Antifašistička Fronta Žena (AFŽ; Antifascist Front of Women) drew together resisters of diverse ideologies.[92] Likewise, the clandestine liberation organization created in Burma in August 1944, at first called the Anti-Fascist Organization and later renamed the Anti-Fascist People's Freedom League, was a difficult and tense coalition effort.[93] The wartime resistance movements preached and generally practiced a politics of unity, drawing on preexisting antifascist solidarities and crafting new ones.

Resistance itself took many forms. The multitude of forms paralleled the multitude of choices people brought themselves to make in difficult

---

[91] Stéphane Courtois, Denis Peschanski, and Adam Rayski, *Le sang de l'étranger: les immigrés de la MOI dans la Résistance* (Paris: Fayard, 1989), 74; Robert Gildea, *Fighters in the Shadows: A New History of the French Resistance* (Cambridge: Belknap Press, 2015), 214–223, 477.

[92] Jelena Batinić, *Women and Yugoslav Partisans: A History of World War II Resistance* (New York: Cambridge University Press, 2015); Gregor Kranj, "Collaboration, Resistance and Liberation in the Balkans, 1941–1945," in *The Cambridge History of the Second World War*, vol. 2: *Politics and Ideology*, eds. Richard J. B. Bosworth and Joseph Maiolo (Cambridge: Cambridge University Press, 2015), 467–469.

[93] Andrew Selth, "Race and Resistance in Burma, 1942–1945," *Modern Asian Studies* 20, no. 3 (1986), 483–507.

circumstances; the crucial choice, though, was to take up resistance, of any sort, in the first place. There were, though, arguments made among antifascists that the form of resistance taken was fundamental to the shape of freedom being created. Umi Sardjono, who took part in the Indonesian antifascist underground, recalled being told by a comrade that the civil disobedience of noncooperation, mass action, and "opposition to fascist colonialism" outweighed acts of armed resistance – "Because," her comrade asked her, "what form do we want independence to take?" Noncooperation, mass action, and anticolonial antifascism, Sardjono was told, generate the democratic ethos needed for republican independence; they ward off nationalism and militarism, the elements of fascism. Sardjono recalled that her comrade concluded, "I approve of all forms of struggle" – as long as they were "democratic and international."[94]

The greatest antifascist example of heroic wartime struggle and resistance was that of the Warsaw Ghetto Uprising of 1943. An act of collective armed resistance, the uprising drew on the general resistance-movement culture that had been built over time by those in the ghetto who had already made the choice to resist, somehow, long before the uprising itself. In a carceral zone where authorities carried out a policy of mass starvation, even getting food past the ghetto's walls depended on elaborate collective smuggling operations. Getting guns was harder. On April 19, 1943, though, hundreds of the Jews confined within the Warsaw Ghetto bravely engaged in (under-)armed resistance against Nazi forces. Doing so drew on many months of organizing. Once the German military occupation of Warsaw had begun, Nazi officials had established the ghetto; they sealed it in November 1940. Within the ghetto, disease and starvation soon spread. In 1941, more than 10 percent of the inhabitants died. In July 1942, the Nazis began carrying out what they called the "Great Action," mass deportation to the Treblinka death camp. In a month's time, the ghetto's population plummeted from 400,000 to fewer than 60,000.[95] By then, resistance within the ghetto had already become collective and organized.

The breakthrough had been four months earlier, with the creation of the Anti-Fascist Bloc. This group had relied on the compromise of

---

[94] Sintha Melati [Umi Sardjono], "In the Service of the Underground: The Struggle Against the Japanese in Java," in *Local Opposition and Underground Resistance to the Japanese in Java, 1942–1945*, ed. Anton Lucas (Melbourne: Centre of Southeast Asian Studies, Monash University, 1986), 139–140.

[95] Israel Gutman, *Resistance: The Warsaw Ghetto Uprising* (Boston: Houghton Mifflin, 1994), xvii.

ideologically diverse factions.[96] One of the organizers described the Anti-Fascist Bloc as "a common front" established on "an agreed program to fight against Fascism and the Nazi occupying power." Another of the organizers identified three aims for the group's "joint forces": "a political and propaganda war against Fascism and reactionary forces within the ghetto," the organization of "anti-Fascist combat divisions" to connect with resistance movements outside the ghetto, and the provision of relief "for the victims of the war against Fascism."[97] At the time of its founding, the Anti-Fascist Bloc's arsenal consisted of one pistol.[98] Amid Nazi repression, the group soon fell apart, but its ethos and surviving members carried over into another organization established soon thereafter, the organization most closely identified with the uprising.

This was the Jewish Fighting Organization, known well by the acronym drawn from its name in Polish – the ŻOB.[99] As soon as the Great Action began, most of the main resistance organizations in the ghetto held urgent meetings to tie their fates together by establishing the ŻOB and committing to the choice of collective armed resistance. "Jewish masses," declared a ŻOB manifesto, "the hour is drawing near. You must be prepared to resist."[100] When Nazi forces moved in to liquidate the ghetto on the morning of April 19, 1943, the ŻOB struck. The armed resistance held out for almost a month, with women and men alike waging urban guerrilla warfare. Casualties were high, and the Nazis eventually razed the ghetto. And yet as one of the ŻOB's great organizers, Marek Edelman, wrote in his 1945 memoir: "One can hardly speak of victories when Life itself is the reason for the fight and so many people are lost, but one thing can surely be stated about this particular battle: we did not let the Germans carry out their plans. They did not evacuate a single living person."[101]

Edelman and others from the uprising carried on their resistance. Edelman even took part in the citywide uprising a year later. Aside from further armed resistance, though, survivors of the Warsaw Ghetto also took up memorial resistance. They knew that there was great ideological power in the stories they had to tell of their memories of armed resistance.

---

[96] Yitzhak Zuckerman ("Antek"), *A Surplus of Memory: Chronicle of the Warsaw Ghetto Uprising*, trans. Barbara Harshav (Berkeley: University of California Press, 1993), 181–184.
[97] Yisrael Gutman, *The Jews of Warsaw, 1939–1943: Ghetto, Underground, Revolt*, trans. Ina Friedman (Bloomington: Indiana University Press, 1982), 171.
[98] Gutman, *Resistance*, 113.
[99] Gutman, *Jews of Warsaw*, 175. The acronym ŻOB was short for Żydowska Organizacja Bojowa.
[100] Gutman, *Resistance*, viii.
[101] Marek Edelman, *The Ghetto Fights* (London: Bookmarks, 1990), 83.

Edelman's writing of his memoir was one such act of memorial resistance. And other antifascists taking part in the war also began almost immediately to memorialize and mythologize the Warsaw Ghetto Uprising. Partisans in Vilna sang a song inspired by it, the song that would become known as the "song of the Warsaw Ghetto," "Zog Nit Keynmol." The partisan, and poet, Hirsh Glik had written it already while the uprising was still ongoing, by the end of May Day 1943.[102] More memorial acts followed. On April 19, 1945 – still before VE Day – ŻOB organizers took part in the presentation of a memorial stone in Warsaw.[103]

A grander memorial at a site that had been part of the ghetto was unveiled on April 19, 1948, designed by the sculptor Natan Rapoport: the Monument to the Ghetto Heroes. It attracted the immediate fascination of antifascists around the world. In Melbourne, Australia, the Jewish antifascist magazine *Unity* repeatedly featured thoughtful discussion of the monument. The historian Max Kaiser argues that the monument drew out a double consciousness for Jewish antifascists in Melbourne. Rapoport's sculpture has two faces, one of heroism and resistance and the other of suffering and victimization. It is a call to remember both the Holocaust and its resistance. The sculpture also signaled to Melbourne's Jewish antifascists a marker of double identity, as Jews and as antifascists, both identities meaningful and each in dialogue with the other.

A doubleness of another sort was at work in the intellectual reception given to the Warsaw monument by Melbourne's Jewish antifascists, a doubled temporality drawing together past and present. By the time that the monument was raised, the Second World War was almost three years over. *Unity* was closely linked to a local organization named the Jewish Council to Combat Fascism and Anti-Semitism, which had been established during the war, in 1942. Like the Junta de la Victoria in Buenos Aires, it had waged the antifascist war far from the front lines. Also like the Junta de la Victoria, it then continued its work after the war ended. *Unity* only began publication in 1948. Its coverage of the Monument to the Ghetto Heroes was among its first acts. By that point, local conservatives had already become critical of the Jewish Council to Combat Fascism and Anti-Semitism for holding onto the name it had first taken during the war. The organization's leader, Aaron Mushin, issued a spirited letter in response, saying, "while Hitler is dead his devilish work lives on in

---

[102] Shirli Gilbert, *Music in the Holocaust: Confronting Life in the Nazi Ghettos and Camps* (Oxford: Clarendon Press, 2005), 70–72.

[103] Zuckerman, *Surplus of Memory*, 676.

those quarters where the refugee, the newcomer, the foreigner, the alien, or the Jew are regarded as something inferior, ... something to be used as a scapegoat."[104]

Mushin's letter spoke to the paramount argument made by antifascists after the Second World War's end. Fascism remained alive, and so the fight against it continued. This was antifascists' fundamental claim everywhere. Partisans in northern Italy kept waging a murderous antifascist war well past 1945. Even after the Third Reich's surrender, in the unoccupied parts of Germany, locals who had taken part in underground resistance during the war now created antifascist committees to organize food distribution (and to punish Nazis) and even to seize local power and carry out little social revolutions according to antifascist principles. These committees, such as the Antifaschistischer Volksausschuß ("Antifascist People's Committee") in Dresden, became known collectively as the antifas, like the two Weimar-era Antifas founded in Berlin or the Antifa-Komiteen of mid-1930s Copenhagen or the Antifa of its contemporary Palestine.[105] In Burma, the coalition effort that had been the face of opposition to the Japanese occupation, the Anti-Fascist People's Freedom League, after the war became the country's most popular – even hegemonic – political party, focused now on fending off British domination. It pointedly kept its antifascist name. In London, Jewish veterans of the war organized the 43 Group in 1946 to shut down fascist street meetings by force.[106] Fascist activity was continuous, and so antifascist resistance was continued.

Such stress on continuity across 1945 ran through the pages of the Melbourne magazine, *Unity*. Memory was at the center of the Jewish Council's politics, but it was not memory from a remove. Quite the opposite, it was memory as a political act of resistance, in the present, against the prevailing narrative that the war – wholesale, not only the war against the Axis but also the war against fascism – was over and had been won. Against the self-satisfied claims that fascism was history, the antifascist argument of continuity framed history not as past but as a tying together of past and present. And the present couldn't be complacent. When the world-famous singer, and Black antifascist, Paul Robeson began singing

---

[104] Max Kaiser, *Jewish Antifascism and the False Promise of Settler Colonialism* (Cham, Switzerland: Palgrave Macmillan, 2022), 28–46, 62.

[105] Wolfgang Leonhard, *Die Revolution entläßt ihre Kinder* (Köln: Kiepenheuer & Witsch, 1955), 250; Gareth Pritchard, *Niemandsland: A History of Unoccupied Germany, 1944–1945* (Cambridge: Cambridge University Press, 2012).

[106] Morris Beckman, *The 43 Group* (London: Centerprise, 1992), 31. See also Daniel Sonabend, *We Fight Fascists: The 43 Group and Their Forgotten Battle for Post-war Britain* (London: Verso, 2019).

the song of the Warsaw Ghetto Uprising, the Yiddish-language "Zog Nit Keynmol," after the war, he began the song with the English-language translation: "Never say that you have reached the very end."

This claim of continuity across 1945 – which, again, pulsed through antifascist discourse all over after the war – speaks to the magnitude of difference between the antifascist conceptions of history and the more typical, nationally centered and normative, conceptions of it. To see 1945 not as a definitive caesura in modern political history but rather as a saddle point in an era that continued well past it – such a perspective, disorienting and startling, full of imaginative possibility, is exemplary of the type of insights to be found in the act of thinking through antifascism's history, guided along by a sense of antifascist praxis.

For the historiography of fascism, by contrast, 1945 has served as the ultimate break point, even at times as the end of fascism's history altogether. For Paxton, in "The Five Stages of Fascism," it's something even more epochal, a superhistorical point of conclusion, when the developmental cycle of his definitive fascist ideal had run its course. By the beginning of the Second World War, Paxton argues, fascism had entered its fifth and final stage, "radicalization or entropy." Here's where his compound ideal of Italian Fascism and German Nazism splits apart. The Mussolini regime, he argues, had largely "subsided toward routine authoritarianism" (though its radicalism then "reappeared at the end of the war in the phantom Republic of Salo"). Meanwhile, "Nazi Germany alone experienced full radicalization." Wartime Nazism provided "the fullest means of expression" of fascist radicalization: exterminatory warmaking, "almost limitless freedom of action," release from "constraints of the 'normative state,'" "ultimate fantasies of racial cleansing." Then, "the humiliating defeat of Hitler."[107] But for Paxton, when the war ended, fascism hadn't simply been defeated; its fixed social-scientific structure had reached its terminus. The model simply ended. Fascism had nowhere to go.

In those years that immediately followed the war, though, antifascist resistance was an argument, in real time, against any post-fascist reading of the postwar present. The argument itself was an act of resistance against the dominant notion of the day that fascism was dead. And so the idea of situating 1945 not as an age's end but rather at an age's center is just the sort of counterintuitive and generative suggestion that I had in mind in this work's introduction when I suggested that you might read what was to follow as an epistemological experiment for rethinking the history of

---

[107] Paxton, "Five Stages of Fascism," 20–22.

fascism through a formulation of antifascism's history. The antifascist history can function diagnostically for fascist history.

Beyond the specific point about 1945, there is also the more general and theoretically quite significant point implicit in the argument that Mushin of Melbourne had made in response to those who suggested that he and his comrades ought to lay down their struggle against fascism. Mushin's response spoke to a grand conception of history that looped together past and present and that gave him a way of understanding the possibilities of the present – possibilities toward a future of his hopes – by keeping up a reckoning with the past. The antifascist philosopher Ewa Majewska, who lives in Warsaw, relates just such a conception of history when she reflects on walking the city, seeing its monuments to the Jews of the Nazi ghetto. The monuments put her in a state of "wonder," she explains, and she laments that the monuments for the uprising are out of synch with the modes of memory generally being produced today in Poland. She contrasts the cultural hegemony of today's Polish nationalist right against the sort of "passionate antifascist education" that she once received, and that she finds still hidden in plain sight in the city's now-old memorials to those who were once confined in the ghetto and resisted.[108]

Part of the Melbourne Jewish antifascists' engagement in the late 1940s with the question of the wartime past's relation to their postwar present concerned the debates then taking shape regarding the conceptualization of genocide. *Unity* paid close attention to the campaign within the United Nations to legislate a convention on the question of genocide. The Polish Jewish jurist Raphael Lemkin had originated the concept during the war and then afterward was pushing for the United Nations to endow it with international governmental authority. Like antifascists elsewhere, Melbourne's plunged into the struggle to make the concept of genocide meaningful – and to shape its meaning. This, of course, was related to the Melbourne antifascists' struggle to establish the historical meaningfulness, and to shape the historical meaning, of the Holocaust. They sought to sharpen the general public's recognition of the antisemitic nature of the Holocaust; and they sought too to define genocide as a general concept, applicable beyond projects driven by antisemitism, the enactment of which could endanger anyone and all. It was argued in the pages of *Unity* that although "the term *genocide*" was fashioned by Lemkin in application "to the crimes committed by the Germans on the civilian population during

---

[108] Ewa Majewska, *Feminist Antifascism: Counterpublics of the Common* (London: Verso, 2012), 16–17.

the war," it still remained so that "genocide itself was not invented by the Nazis; the blood-stained history of our planet contains dreadful chapters on the mass extermination of human beings."[109] Such logic had startling ramifications for Melbourne's Jewish antifascists. The generalization of the genocide concept helped the Melbourne-based Jewish Council as a group to conceive of a politics of solidarity with the contemporary Aboriginal resistance struggles in Australia. That in turn led the group's members to develop a critique of settler colonialism as a meaningful general concept of its own – and to argue that Zionism was a particular manifestation of it.[110] In the years that followed the Second World War, theirs was an ongoing, living, learning, and open-ended antifascism.

The same was true of Paul Robeson's antifascism in the postwar years. In December 1951, he presented to the United Nations, on Manhattan Island, a text charging genocide by the United States government against its Black citizens. Robeson did so on behalf of an antifascist organization to which he was deeply committed, the Civil Rights Congress (CRC). The group also had the text published as a book: *We Charge Genocide*. Part of the CRC's originality lay in the text's argument that "genocide leads to fascism" instead of only the other way around. What's more, in the hands of the CRC, the dynamic of genocide was profoundly transnational, as when the group pointed to "Hitler's demonstration that genocide at home can become wider massacre abroad, that domestic genocide develops into the larger genocide that is predatory war." The signatories of *We Charge Genocide* declared bluntly: "Jellied gasoline in Korea and the lynchers' faggot at home are connected in more ways than that both result in death by fire. The lyncher and the atom bomber are related."[111]

After the *We Charge Genocide* affair, Robeson went on to dedicate much of his antifascist labor to the defeat of apartheid in South Africa. His main vehicle of antifascist solidarity with the people of South Africa was another organization to which he was deeply committed, the Council on African Affairs. Based in New York, the group focused on fighting colonialism, fascism, and white supremacy. Robeson took part in making the Council's haunting 1951 documentary *South Africa – Uncensored* and

---

[109] Simon Wolf, "Genocide: The Crime That Is No Longer Nameless," *Unity: A Magazine of Jewish Affairs* 2, no. 3 (Sept. 1949), 13; Kaiser, *Jewish Antifascism and the False Promise of Settler Colonialism*, 47.

[110] Kaiser, *Jewish Antifascism and the False Promise of Settler Colonialism*, esp. 230–251.

[111] William L. Patterson, ed., *We Charge Genocide: The Historic Petition to the United Nations for Relief from a Crime of the United States Government against the Negro People* (New York: Civil Rights Congress, 1951), 3, 7.

performed as the film's narrator. The group publicized the documentary as a "powerful education weapon" showing "why the struggle against S. African fascism directly concerns us Americans." An antifascist film, it was also specifically antigenocidal, drawing critical connections between the violence of contemporary South Africa and the Nazi concentration camps of the Third Reich era as well as the early twentieth-century imperial German genocide of the Herero and Nama in German South-West Africa – a "war of extermination," Robeson narrates.[112] Early in 1952, writing in the reliably brilliant and militant newsletter put out by the Council, *Spotlight on Africa*, Robeson laid out for his readers a thoroughly antifascist argument for solidarity with the people of South Africa: The apartheid regime is intrinsically fascist and the African National Congress (ANC) is resolutely antifascist, so commit yourself to solidarity with the ANC; doing so will not only aid the ANC in its righteous cause but also will teach you how to wage an antifascist struggle of your own, even as you in turn inspire others elsewhere; it is by such catalytic acts of solidarity and resistance that the worldwide struggle against fascism is made.[113]

Robeson and the rest of the Council on African Affairs were fashioning a theoretically intricate conceptualization of fascism in history. Fascism, c. 1952, as theorized by the Council, operated in two different temporal domains. One was of linear continuity with pre-1945 fascism, of the sort that Aaron Mushin had depicted. The other operated as a realm of pre-1945 fascism's reenactment. In the first case, not all the fascists had been defeated in 1945, and so now seven years later there still abounded long-familiar fascists who simply continued the work that they, and others, had begun well before 1945. In the second case, neo-fascists sought a mystical return to the past, to channel it and to reenact it in the present so as to give it a different ending in the future. So, according to the notion of continuity, it was no surprise to *Spotlight on Africa* that the apartheid regime currently working to impose "fascist enslavement" in postwar South Africa was led by a man, the right-wing Afrikaner nationalist Daniël François Malan, who had been "an ardent supporter of Hitler" while Hitler had lived. Also, though, according to the notion of fascism's

---

[112] *Spotlight on Africa* 11, no. 5 (April 14, 1952), 2; *South Africa – Uncensored* (1951). The film is available for streaming at "South Africa Uncensored," *Smithsonian National Museum of African American History and Culture*, https://nmaahc.si.edu/object/nmaahc_2012.79.1.5.1a#. Accessed Dec. 10, 2024.

[113] Paul Robeson, "An Important Message from Paul Robeson," *Spotlight on Africa* 11, no. 2 (Feb. 25, 1952), 1.

reenactment, it was no surprise to *Spotlight* that the Malan regime had "defied the United Nations and stolen South West Africa," because, after all, "Fascist Italy" had in 1935 "defied the League of Nations and raped Ethiopia." The apartheid regime's expansionist hunger was the revival of fascism at its most ravenous. It was, the Council warned, a replay of the Nazi policy of "Lebensraum."[114]

Not only did antifascism pulse within the politics of those who expressed solidarity with the people of South Africa from afar; among those who waged the liberation struggle within the country, as well, there were strong antifascist commitments.[115] On April 6, 1952, to publicize the "plan of action" for the upcoming Defiance Campaign, the ANC put on rallies throughout the country. The Johannesburg rally at Freedom Square in Fordsburg was a fiery event. Nelson Mandela spoke, as did the experienced organizer of passive resistance Yusuf Mohamad Dadoo, on behalf of the South African Indian Congress. Dadoo declared: "We say to Dr. Malan we will not allow fascism in South Africa. Fascism can only come over our dead bodies."[116]

Antifascism remained a part of the South African liberation struggle. When *Sechaba* was launched as the ANC's new official organ in January 1967, the journal promised, in its first issue, to spread news to the world of "the struggle being waged by the oppressed people of South Africa against fascist apartheid tyranny."[117] The first message of the new journal was a collective statement of purpose, written on behalf of the ANC. The statement announced that the present moment opened a perilous period for South Africa: A historic future was nascent in the present. "History," the statement read, "may well record that *Sechaba* was born on the eve of a violent clash between the freedom forces on the one side and those of racism and fascism on the other." Already the country seemed to be experiencing an undeclared civil war. The oppressed masses had mobilized. Out of desperation, the regime, led by the newly installed premier B. J. Vorster, had engaged in "frantic military preparations," enlisting "virtually every white person in South Africa … in this army to defend

---

[114] "Support the South African People's Campaign Against Fascist Enslavement" and "Does Fascism Rule South Africa? Here Are a Few Facts!" *Spotlight on Africa* 11, no. 2 (Feb. 25, 1952), 2.

[115] See Jonathan Hyslop, Kasper Braskén, and Neil Roos, eds., "Anti-Fascism in Southern Africa," Special Issue, *South African Historical Journal* 74, no. 1 (2022).

[116] "South Africans at Nation-wide April 6 Protest Rallies Pledge All-out Campaign of Defiance against Unjust Laws," *Spotlight on Africa* 11, no. 5 (April 14, 1952), 2.

[117] *Sechaba* (Jan. 1967), 10.

white domination and fascism." The oppressed of the nation, the ANC insisted, "will not submit to Nazi Vorster."[118]

It was 1967 and the antifascist message remained vivid: The fight against fascism had not ended with Nazi Germany's defeat in 1945. Old fascists persisted, and new ones kept coming. The antifascist war continued; the civil war was ongoing and evolving. The fight for freedom remained yet to be won. In the fourth age of antifascist history, antifascists would place freedom at the center of their struggle.

4 The Age of Freedom Antifascism, 1968–1984

"Freedom or fascism" – that was the way Beatriz Allende articulated the terrible predicament of the age. The middle ground, she said, had fallen away. Throughout the years since Hitler's death, fascism had shown its weedlike resilience. Now, Allende argued, where it had been left uneradicated, it was beginning to show its capacity for choking out competing forms of rule. Welfare states, mixed regimes, politics as usual – fascism consumes them all whole in the end. This meant, Allende had decided, that the antifascists of the day had to commit to nothing short of absolute freedom. The equilibrium of the postwar status quo had been illusory; the state of things had shown to be a slide to fascism. And so, she argued, total freedom was the only refuge from the totalitarianism in prospect. When she made the argument, she was speaking to an audience of fellow antifascists in Chicago in July 1974. She was touring to build publicity and support for the transnational movement of solidarity with the people of Chile, a movement that had already become dramatically global in scale in the ten months since the military coup that had ended democratic rule in Chile and had left dead its inspiring socialist president – Beatriz Allende's father, Salvador Allende. The coup, she said, had stripped the people of Chile of any choices other than that of freedom or fascism. What's more, she argued, the coup in Chile was a sign of things to come elsewhere, of fascist futures. The choice before the people of Chile, Allende argued, was the same as that before the people of Chicago, and all over.[119]

For Kathleen Cleaver, it had been clear in 1968 that the only choices left were freedom or fascism. The year before, she had moved to San Francisco to join the Black Panthers Party, and by September 1968, when she issued

---
[118] "Commentary," *Sechaba* (Jan. 1967), 1.
[119] Beatriz Allende, *"... Before the Eyes and Conscience of the World": Beatriz Allende Speaks to the North American People* (New York: Venceremos Brigade, n.d. [1974]), 5.

her prime statement on the dialectic of fascism and freedom, she was a member of the party's Central Committee.[120] In her statement – published as "Racism, Fascism, and Political Murder" in the Panthers' newspaper – Cleaver argued that the recent struggles for Black freedom in the United States had had a diagnostic effect. Their suppression had served as the "most clearly visible" evidence of "the advent of fascism in the United States." Yes, she argued, "the overt military dictatorship is yet to come," but its methods of domination were "already started on a sporadic scale in the spontaneous but condoned murdering of young black men in the streets daily all over the country." She argued that "an outright fascist attack on the whole black community" was presently hampered only by the political vicissitudes of an election year and the imperial overreach of military force in Vietnam. Cleaver expected that once the military apparatus was withdrawn from Vietnam, "outright genocide of black people will be initiated" in the United States. The machinery of the genocide was in motion; the level of "intensified and concentrated police power in the black community" aimed at one end: "to impose total control." Black people's options had been reduced to two: "FREEDOM OR DEATH." The argument was like the one Allende would offer six years later: freedom or fascism, or, as Cleaver also put it, "total liberation or total extinction."[121]

The world-spanning social explosions of 1968 delivered one era's end and announced another's inception. The politics of the new era were, from the start, unsettling and full of subversive intuition and experimentation. The unsettlement and subversion came to involve the reworking and the rearticulation of key concepts of global politics, concepts such as autonomy, democracy, and human rights. The concepts that stand out as keys to the age, though, were those of freedom and liberation.[122] And it was on these two very – deeply related – concepts, along with the concept of fascism, that the antifascists of the age had the most to say. I say that "the antifascists" had the most to say, but in 1968 and the years that followed what was most striking about the dramatis personae of antifascism was that new – and young – practitioners wrote their names onto antifascism's list of role players. Much more emphatically than their elders

---

[120] Joshua Bloom and Waldo E. Martin, Jr., *Black Against Empire: The History and Politics of the Black Panther Party* (Oakland: University of California Press, 2013), 105–107.
[121] Kathleen Cleaver, "Racism, Fascism, and Political Murder," *Black Panther*, September 14, 1968, p. 8.
[122] Michael Hardt, *The Subversive Seventies* (New York: Oxford University Press, 2023), 9, 10, 293 *n*17.

did, the youthful activists of the New Left in these years drove antifascist politics. The newly engaged and the young became antifascists as they went, as they worked out their ideas and as they practiced their politics. This, of course, was more or less the same way that antifascists had been made in ages past: step by step, through political work. The new initiates theorized fascism and disputed their own and others' theorizations; they revised their theories and took from others'; they called out and confronted and tried to smash (what they theorized to be) fascism. They did these things, not necessarily in that order. Antifascism was done on the fly: As the examples of Allende and Cleaver would suggest, the theorization of fascism in these years was an urgent affair, very much an engaged political act – a part of the freedom project.

The age's retheorizations of fascism centered on the state.[123] Both Cleaver and Allende targeted the state with their own theorizations, and in this their line of thinking ran parallel to that of others of the age. There were differences, though, in Cleaver's and Allende's theories of the fascist state.

With her 1968 statement on fascism ("Racism, Fascism, and Political Murder"), Cleaver opened a period of insistent and intricate theorizing of fascism carried out by members of the Black Panthers Party – through which, along with their other defiant acts against fascism, the Panthers made themselves into thoroughgoing antifascists. Along the way, they also inspired others to follow their example, very much in the way that Paul Robeson had imagined that the worldwide antifascist struggle could take flight when he had praised the inspirational example of the South African freedom fight. The theories of state fascism that were worked out in the Panthers' discourse built on Cleaver's depiction of a "sporadic scale" of fascism at work within the state's machinery. The imperious violence of the police in Black ghettoes, the imperialist striving in Vietnam, the demagoguery of white supremacist politicians, the economic imperilment of the lumpenproletariat, the unrestrained terrorization of those who organized protest, and the insatiate drive toward mass incarceration: these were dynamics generated from within the increasingly panicked (and decreasingly) liberal state.

Beatriz Allende's theorization of fascism, as well as the theorizations of fascism made by others in the Chilean solidarity movement, centered on what she, and they, saw as the ultimate fascist act-form in the acquisition

---

[123] See, for example, Nicos Poulantzas, *Fascisme et dictature: la IIIe Internationale face au fascisme* (Paris: Maspéro, 1970).

of power: the coup d'état (or, in Spanish, "el golpe"). The coup that had ended with General Augusto Pinochet holding dictatorial power over Chile was a military coup, but it was as much to Allende's point that it was a militarists' coup. And an exclusionary nationalists' coup and a terroristic antileftists' coup. That is, it wasn't a coup carried out by apolitical military authorities acting to save the country from ideology. It was a coup carried out by ideologically driven political actors, ideological actors who were quick to propagate a politics of hatred toward their enemies and chosen scapegoats. The act-form of the coup was not a method that they had just happened upon, being military men; rather, the coup was indicative and generative of the ideological order they sought to impose.

The idea of the coup d'état as the quintessential fascist route to power was, and is, far from settled theoretical ground. In "The Five Stages of Fascism," Paxton puts stress on an opposing argument, based on his claim that "neither Hitler nor Mussolini took the helm by force." The point is important for his theme of conservative collaboration with fascists. In both the cases of Hitler and Mussolini, Paxton argues, the eventual dictators first acquired power by legitimate means, by even somewhat obscure and procedural means situated as if at a remove from the rough and tumble of politics. For Paxton, what's significant about this is that the fascists' acquisitions of power in Italy and Germany were enabled by conservative elites who hoped that they could both manage the fascists and make use of them to suppress popular mobilizations and "an advancing Left." Paxton then goes on to repurpose his historical reading of Mussolini's and Hitler's acquisitions of state power as a transhistorical axiom: "The only route to power available to fascists passes through cooperation with conservative elites." He has two reasons for making this absolute claim. First, here, as with other aspects of his argument, he has generalized the particular historical examples of Mussolini-era Fascism and Hitler-era Nazism into universal rules of fascism's definition. Second, he argues as a point of logic that "fascist power by coup is hardly conceivable in a modern state" because "fascism cannot appeal to the street without risking a confrontation with future allies – the army and the police." He does not take up the question of what might happen if the fascism in question *were* the army or the police. Nor does Paxton address the case of the Pinochet dictatorship in some other fashion. Rather, he suggests, in his essay (published in 1998), "We need to recall that fascism has never so far taken power by a coup d'état."[124] The historical claim embedded in the declarative

---

[124] Paxton, "Five Stages of Fascism," 16, 17.

statement is a good example of what makes me wary of Paxton's general method. (Interestingly, though, this particular claim of Paxton's implies an openness to something new and different happening in the future of fascist history – the statement that fascism "so far" hasn't taken power by coup seems to imply that it could happen in the future. Which is to say: Paxton's mode of thought here is quite different from when he pronounces a transhistorical axiom.) The problem here, as I see it, is that Paxton's historical claim (even as open-minded as it is about the future) is based on a definition of fascism that is itself closed to revision – in the case of the acquisition of state power (Paxton's Stage Three), closed to revision after January 1933. (As always with Paxton's stagist model, that temporal enclosure is connected to the spatial enclosure: Once the Fascist Italian and Nazi German examples are given a monopoly on defining fascism, then obviously that definition is closed to revision from outside of Europe in the same way it's closed to any temporal point post-VE Day; either way, Chile 1973 is out.) The reason for Paxton's definitional claims is to provide structure for the comparison as a way of thinking that guides his essay. The purpose of the closed definition is to afford comparison of other episodes in history against the closed definition.

Cleaver's theory of state fascism is radically different from Paxton's interpretation; it also differs substantially from Allende's theory of state fascism. Significantly, the theorization given by Cleaver, and those given by the Panthers who followed her, doesn't hinge on the act of coup d'état. Rather, Cleaver's notion of state fascism suggests a gradual and, at least initially, surreptitious capture of the state. Fascism hadn't acquired state power so much as state power had acquired fascism. But, for Cleaver, this had happened, or was happening, step by step, not all at once. In the United States, the "overt military dictatorship," she said, remained in 1968 still a fascist future, a fascist "not-yet." Genocide, she said, had not yet commenced. What had commenced was that Black people who resisted the fascist creep were "being jailed, framed, shot, murdered, eliminated." These actions were "setting the stage for genocide."[125]

By July 1969, when the Black Panthers Party held the era's great antifascist mass gathering, the National Conference for a United Front against Fascism in America, the Panthers had established antifascism as one of their core principles. Held in Oakland, the conference had the aim of unifying the nation's radical movements, and then eventually the nation's masses, to "oppose fascism in action, where it counts," in practice. The

---

[125] Cleaver, "Racism, Fascism, and Political Murder," p. 8.

Panthers' call to attend the conference stated, "Every man, woman or child dehumanized by the 'culture' of imperialism has to be anti-fascist."[126]

The main practical effect of the conference was to launch the Panthers' multiracial community-based organizing effort, the National Committees to Combat Fascism (NCCFs). Several local branches were already established in cities such as New York, Los Angeles, and Chicago before the conference, but the gathering all the same functioned as the launchpad for a properly national network of local chapters. The NCCFs were community-based collectivities that mounted everyday antifascism from the bottom up, with the aim of countering the everyday fascist drip from above.

In contrast to Cleaver's rendering of the sporadically fascist state was Allende's emphasis on the fascist seizure of state power by coup d'état. At least arguably, the defining act of fascism in this age of freedom antifascism was the military coup in Chile, and, likewise, at least arguably, the defining cause of antifascism in the age was that of transnational solidarity with the people of Chile suffering under the dictatorship that followed the coup.[127] The solidarity movement was global, explicitly and emphatically antifascist, and driven by very antifascist conceptions of unity, solidarity, and freedom.

Pinochet and his fellow golpistas had carried out the coup on September 11, 1973. Before the month was out, Beatriz Allende was in Havana, announcing the solidarity movement's inception in a speech in the Plaza de la Revolución. She described her father as having determined, on September 11, "to fight to the end without surrendering to the treasonous military, whom he already called by their true names – fascists."[128] In her speech, Allende said that when she last saw her father, on September 11 shortly before he died, he told her that the unfolding day constituted not an end but a beginning, "the beginning of a long resistance." Her biographer Tanya Harmer suggests that it was in making her speech into such a "call to action" – rather than an elegy alone – that Allende stepped into a "new life as a leader of the resistance to Chile's dictatorship."[129]

---

[126] "The Black Panther Party Calls for a United Front Against Fascism," *Black Panther*, June 28, 1969, p. 20.

[127] On the influence of the solidarity movement, see Kim Christiaens, "European Reconfigurations of Transnational Activism: Solidarity and Human Rights Campaigns on Behalf of Chile during the 1970s and 1980s," *International Review of Social History* 63, no. 3 (Dec. 2018), 413–448.

[128] *The Highest Example of Heroism* (Havana: Instituto Cubano del Libro, 1973), 17.

[129] *Highest Example of Heroism*, 13, 21–23; Tanya Harmer, *Beatriz Allende: A Revolutionary Life in Cold War Latin America* (Chapel Hill: University of North Carolina Press, 2020), 218.

Two weeks later, Allende established the antifascist organization she would lead for the next four years, the Comité Chileno de Solidaridad con la Resistencia Antifascista. The committee played a central role in the transnational movement of solidarity with Chile that, in turn, played a central role in antifascist politics as a whole during the age of freedom antifascism. The Comité practiced a distinct sort of antifascist politics, much of it shaped by Allende. Harmer stresses that Allende came of age at a moment of New Leftist revolutionary ferment among Latin America's young student-intellectuals. As a student, she had fashioned her own singular revolutionary politics, in dialogue with her friends and dear comrades in the Movimiento de Izquierda Revolucionaria (MIR), which was a militant Chilean New Leftist party/movement organization established in 1965; its aims were more radical than her father's ballot-box socialism. The miristas, as the party's adherents are known, pieced together an unruly and participatory politics of revolutionary struggle.

Their politics were expressly antifascist well before the coup of September 11, 1973. During the Allende presidency, miristas shared a general expectation that just such a coup was coming, and they saw themselves as working urgently to bring about the revolution first. Their thinking wasn't developmentalist; they didn't think that domestic Chilean fascism was developing through internal stages toward takeoff. Rather, their rationale came of looking beyond Chile's borders and understanding the world outside of Chile as it was moving in the moment. Fascism, miristas warned as the 1970s began, was a global monstrosity consuming national societies. For miristas, Brazil had already been suffering under a "fascistoid dictatorship" when Bolivia fell to "the fascist military coup" of August 1971.[130] Faced with such an international context, Allende-era miristas argued that the Chilean left had to practice a disciplined antifascist unity and, perhaps counterintuitively, also had to commit to revolutionary socialism to bring about a comprehensively just society before the fascists could intervene. The antifascist principles of Beatriz Allende, who in 1968 had done covert revolutionary work in Bolivia, were more akin to those of the miristas than to those of her father.[131]

The antifascism of Allende's post-coup committee was also akin to that of the Black Panthers. Like the Panthers, the Comité communicated

---

[130] "Golpe fascista: Última advertencia," *Rebelde* (Aug. 28, 1971), 11 (see also issue cover); Hernan Lavin Cerda, "Brasil, repression y tortura," *Punto Final*, June 22, 1971, p. 22; Gonzalo Rodríguez and Tomás Catavi, "Bolivia: Una lección para la izquierda," *Punto Final: Documentos* (supplement), Sept. 14, 1971, pp. 3, 4, 8.

[131] Harmer, *Beatriz Allende*, 102–103, 106.

an understanding of fascism as being fundamentally a regime type. Like the Panthers, the Comité stressed that fascist regimes were machines of repression: They practiced violence to eliminate particular enemies and to terrorize the general public; fascist regimes were the henchmen of imperialism and monopoly capitalism. On all these points, the Panthers and the Comité agreed. Also much like the Panthers, and the miristas, the Comité insisted on antifascist unity, to be enforced by the principle of solidarity, as the ultimate strategic imperative.

Beginning with the first anniversary of the coup, the Comité and other Chilean exile groups made September 11 into an annual worldwide day of mourning and mobilization. Typical of proceedings at the day's commemorative events was to invoke the memory of Salvador Allende and to invest his death with special symbolic meaning. No one could do this better than Beatriz Allende. The day's events didn't only memorialize though; they also accentuated the ongoing fight against fascism and made claims of the Chilean people's ongoing, undimmed antifascist defiance. There was, to be sure, always still an elegiacal feel to the affairs, but such mourning was generally preliminary to expressions of a related but different sadness: The sorrow shared by those displaced, because they now missed their homeland. They wanted to return. They missed home as much as they missed the past. Unlike the mournful remembrances for the martyrs of September 11, that specific sorrow spoke to a wrong that could still be made right.

In her speeches, Beatriz Allende conveyed the compound of mourning, melancholy, sorrow, defiance, determination, and hope shared by Chilean antifascists. When she spoke in Caracas on September 11, 1974, she began by grounding her oratory in a memorial mode but then worked to convert the affective energy of elegy into something ongoing and growing. That is, she worked to subvert the typical elegiac mode of memorial oratory, offering her comrades "a combative message of solidarity" in an hour "of pain, but also of hope." She went on to say: "Today we remember all those who fight fascism."[132] *Fight* – present tense. With this, Allende had cleverly shifted the speech from an act of mourning for the departed to an act of commitment to those who fought on still in Chile, even after the forced departure of exiles such as herself. Instead of we-remember-the-dead, the speech now meant we-remember-those-who(-now)-fight, or, more to the point, we-remember-to-fight.

---

[132] "Mensaje de Beatriz Allende al pueblo chileno," *Granma*, Sept. 11, 1974, p. 2.

Typical of such memorial oratory was Allende's suggestion that her father's "last words are with us" in the present, prodding onward those who fight. But typical of antifascist argumentation was that she also argued that it is the heroism of those who struggle in the present that gives the President's words added significance, new life. It was *because* of the ongoing resistance within Chile that people of goodwill throughout the world now, on this day, took care to remember her father. Yes, martyrs such as her father remained in the hearts of those who fought on and, as such, gave a gift from the grave. But it was more to Allende's point that the past is given meaning by the struggles of the present. It was because of "our struggle" in the now that "everywhere TODAY President Allende and all those who fought in our country" – *fought*, past tense – "will be remembered."[133] Again, quite typical of the antifascism of the age, past and present danced together in Allende's argument.

That same day, demonstrations of solidarity with the people of Chile took place in cities throughout the world, including but not limited to Lima, Buenos Aires, Bogotá, Mexico City, London, Paris, Bonn, East Berlin, Rome, Cairo, Jerusalem, Moscow, Ulaanbaatar, and Tokyo.[134] More demonstrations followed in the years that followed. Local spadework added up, and the solidarity movement as a whole amounted to one of the great causes in antifascist history.

More broadly, the era's antifascist critiques of state power, and its theorizations of the ways – by coup or by creeping – that a state might become fascist, constituted a significant contribution to antifascist history. In particular, these critiques constituted a significant contribution to the antifascists' ongoing project of conceptualizing fascism so as to fight it more effectively. And so antifascist theorizations drawn from the era, such as those of Kathleen Cleaver and the other Black Panthers and Beatriz Allende and the Comité Chileno de Solidaridad con la Resistencia Antifascista, might well be used to open the history of fascism well beyond the specific examples handed down from Mussolini's Italy or Hitler's Germany. In light of the theorizations made during the age of freedom antifascism, the very question of fascism's acquisition of state power could

---

[133] "Mensaje de Beatriz Allende al pueblo chileno," p. 2.
[134] "Actividades de solidaridad con la lucha del pueblo de Chile como parle de la gran jornada internacional," *Granma*, Sept. 7, 1974, p. 1; "Prosigue desarrollandose en todo el mundo la jornada internacional de solidaridad con la lucha del pueblo chileno contra el fascismo," *Granma*, Sept. 10, 1974, p. 1; "Celebran numerosas actividades en todo el mundo en solidaridad con la lucha del pueblo chileno contra el fascismo," *Granma*, Sept. 12, 1974, p. 1.

easily be seen as too narrowly constructed by Paxton. In the hands of the Black Panthers, the state instead appears a locus of fascism's becoming. In the hands of Allende, the enactment of a coup d'état comes off as not at all a fixed reason to conclude that its enactors are by definition not fascist – because Mussolini and Hitler didn't gain state power by coup. The enactment of a coup becomes, rather, very much a practice that can both indicate and generate fascism. After all, if Hitler's Beer Hall Putsch had succeeded, would that have meant that he wasn't a fascist? Or, rather, was that episode, even in failure, for Hitler and his movement a generative breakthrough, a mythmaking, commitment-cementing, and identity-forging rite of passage?

A final point, regarding the antifascists' flipside of fascist dictatorship: antifascist freedom. Throughout the age of freedom antifascism, antifascists loudly condemned fascist dictatorships, and they also experimented in their praxis to figure out alternative forms of social organization, better and more just and free forms. One form that drew antifascist experimentation throughout the era was that of the commune. For a variety of antifascists at the time, communing was a way of cutting a path away from one of fascism's key components, nationalism; it was a way of getting away from the national form altogether, along with authoritarian rule, militarism and the imperial temptation, and the alienation typical of mass society.

In this, as in their antifascist critique of the state, Black Panthers threw one of the first punches. In November 1970, Huey Newton gave a famous speech in which he laid out not only an idea of communal life but also an idea of its power to prefigure an alternative world order that leaves nations and nationalism behind. Newton depicted his proposal as "revolutionary intercommunalism." By January 1971, a group of Black Panthers had announced a revolutionary commune, named for a martyr "murdered by reactionary fascist pigs," Jonathan P. Jackson. The commune was to be a radically transformative endeavor. "The J. P. J. Commune," its founders wrote, "will seek through its activities to totally transform all the negative qualities that the system has imbued and programmed into our brothers into positive forms." The first communards declared themselves "anti-capitalist, anti-imperialist, anti-colonialist, anti-racist, and anti-fascist." They freely expected to make mistakes – and to learn from them. They promised to "set revolutionary examples so that others may follow" and to act as "brothers who are willing to learn and to teach each other the meaning of being a true revolutionary." What was most revolutionary about the J. P. J.'s experimentation in liberation was that the commune itself was founded inside Sing Sing, the notorious New York state prison – or as the communards called it, the "New York State Concentration Camp."[135] The J. P. J. Communards were all imprisoned men. Other Panthers also drew on the idea of imagining communal freedom directly out of places of fascist unfreedom. Monk Teba of the Panthers' Illinois chapter compared Chicago's Cabrini Green Housing Projects to the Nazis' Warsaw Ghetto but, perhaps thinking of the uprising of 1943, suggested that resistance was necessary to transform oppression into freedom as a catalytic example for bringing about "the whole world global commune."[136]

Other antifascist communes followed.

Only weeks after the J. P. J. Commune was announced in the *Black Panther*, radical students at the University of the Philippines Diliman in Quezon City threw up barricades and declared the campus a commune in the spirit of the Paris Commune 100 years past. The barricading of campus took place amid national turmoil; the previous month had been consumed by rumors of coups d'état and fears that President Ferdinand Marcos would declare martial law and seize dictatorial powers. The students who barricaded campus declared it "liberated." They took over a radio station with the power to transmit to the entire Philippine archipelago.[137] In a message "to all Diliman Communards," the commune's provisional directorate thanked everyone involved for "in the heroic defense of the Diliman Commune against the fascist military of the Marcos regime." The directorate also warned the communards to guard against the university administration's "hirelings" who "mouth fascist anti-student slogans."[138] The Diliman Commune maintained its state of liberation for nine days. Afterward, the efficacy of the affair became the topic of considerable debate, though those who took part didn't doubt its pedagogical effect. Their critique of the government prefigured the antifascist rhetoric that ensued the following year, when Marcos did declare martial law and assume dictatorial powers. Mass detentions, systematic torture, and disappearances followed.[139]

---

[135] "Brothers in New York State Concentration Camp Form the Jonathan P. Jackson Commune," *Black Panther*, Jan. 9, 1971, p. 8.
[136] Monk Teba, "Cabrini Green Housing Projects … the Same as the Warsaw Ghetto of Poland in 1942," *Black Panther*, Dec. 14, 1970, p. 5.
[137] Joseph Scalice, *The Drama of Dictatorship: Martial Law and the Communist Parties of the Philippines* (Ithaca: Southeast Asia Program Publications, 2023), 110–138.
[138] "To All Diliman Communards," *Bandilang Pula*, Feb. 12, 1971, p. B.
[139] *Report of an Amnesty International Mission to The Republic of the Philippines, 22 November-5 December 1975* (Wembley: Amnesty International Publications, 1976).

In 1979, the Turkish antifascist movement Devrimci Yol carried out a communard experiment in the city of Fatsa, on the Black Sea coast. Antifascist ideals animated the Fatsa Commune, and antifascist organizing practices had prompted the circumstances of its creation. As the political theorist Michael Hardt explains, "Antifascist struggle was the central pillar of Devrimci Yol's program, and, indeed, fascist violence was an extraordinarily widespread and pressing threat in Turkey" at the 1970s' end. The main perpetrators of the fascist violence were the Grey Wolves, a paramilitary group that carried out murder and massacre to further its ultranationalist aims. Devrimci Yol created self-defense-oriented "resistance committees" with a strong antifascist ethos to fend off the Grey Wolves. These committees, though, not only fought the Grey Wolves, they also generated lessons of empowerment and political imagination for their grassroots participants. The committees were, Hardt argues, "a gateway ... that opened to democratic participation." That participation blossomed into the experimental democracy that was the Fatsa Commune. In the heady days of the commune's enactment, the committees took direct part in the governing of the city, and members became acutely conscious of themselves as Fatsa's free citizenry. In 1980, the experiment was squashed when the national army marched on Fatsa and imposed a domestic military occupation. A nationwide military coup d'état followed, with a military junta seizing power on September 12, 1980.[140]

And so throughout the age of freedom antifascism experiences of fascist state power and experiments in antifascist freedom were related. One informed the other, and each signified a form of the other's negation.

For all the experimentation of practice and innovation of theory that marked the age, though, it would be a mistake to disregard the dimensions of antifascism in this era that were strikingly consistent with the sorts of politics that antifascists had fashioned in earlier eras. Constancy was apparent most of all in the popular politics of militant confrontation, collective self-defense, and forceful rejection of fascism's sacralization of violence and its racism, antisemitism, and scapegoating, and its idealization of the exclusionary nation to be bludgeoned into existence by a dictatorial state. As in earlier eras, a point that distinguished antifascists from other non-fascists around them, many of whom disliked fascism and voiced criticism of it in passing, was their determination to confront fascism from its point of inception. In Britain, an assortment of longtime fascists and up-and-coming post-fascists and neo-fascists established the

---

[140] Hardt, *Subversive Seventies*, 241–246.

National Front in 1967. White-nationalistic, antisemitic, absorbed by conspiracy theories, and violently hostile to immigrants, the National Front provoked a multipronged, mass-based antifascist response, exemplified by the Anti-Nazi League. The impetus for the Anti-Nazi League came from the "Battle of Lewisham" of 1977, when antifascists broke up a National Front march and defied the police.[141] Somewhat famously, the Anti-Nazi League drew into the ranks of antifascism the politically unengaged by putting on popular cultural events. Less well known is that the Anti-Nazi League also organized squads of militants to derail National Front events. The Anti-Nazi League additionally took up serious interracial antiracist political organizing.[142] The publications *Searchlight* and the *Anti-Fascist Bulletin* helped articulate the era's antifascist discourse. Both stressed the only half-disguised Nazism that infused the National Front's ideas and practices, and both kept their readers informed of the latest antifascist acts of courage.[143] Such acts drew on and distilled what by then was a decades-long legacy of antifascist history. Such acts, though, because they generally were derived from a dense concentration of militant direct action and community-based confrontation, could also be said to have been prefiguring the age to come, the age of antifa.

5 The Antifa Age, since 1985

So it didn't come out of nowhere, but, still, a new age of antifascist history, with its own distinct ethos, could be said to have started taking form in 1985 with the creation of fiercely militant groups such as Anti-Fascist Action in London and the Red Warriors in Paris. These groups were not only militant but also confrontational, provocative, and disciplined. In some ways, they represented a back-to-basics antifascism; their emphasis on collective self-defense and unflinching, often violent, confrontation with fascists was not only akin to more recent and closer-to-home actions of the sort documented in *Searchlight* and the *Anti-Fascist Bulletin* but also akin to the core praxis of groups from farther afield and further in the past: groups such as the Arditi del Popolo or the Antifaschistische Junge Garde – the original Antifa. By targeting fascists in action out in the public arena – in particular

---

[141] Nigel Copsey, *Anti-Fascism in Britain*, second edition (London: Routledge, 2017), 119–135.

[142] Paul Gilroy, *There Ain't No Black in the Union Jack: The Cultural Politics of Race and Nation* (1987; Milton Park, Abingdon: Routledge, 2002), 148, 170–177; Sean Birchall, *Beating the Fascists: The Untold Story of Anti-Fascist Action* (London: Freedom Press, 2010), 35–44.

[143] For example, *Anti-Fascist Bulletin*, no. 5 (Mar. 1971), 7.

those readily identifiable, out-and-out fascists agitating and glowering in the streets and public squares – the new generation of antifascists that came on the scene c. 1985 offered blunt and forceful takes on familiar antifascist themes. At the same time, the new generation worked out in practice more or less the sorts of antifascism that have been stressed in the twenty-first century and that have generally drawn the label "antifa" – oftentimes drawing that label even more readily than they've drawn the historically broader term "antifascism." Today in the twenty-first century, antifa has become a keyword (and scare word) of contemporary global politics, a contested and volatile – and all the same critical – concept. The conception of antifa that is ascendant today has its roots in the Antifaschistische Junge Garde and Antifaschistische Aktion of Weimar-era Germany; it owes a debt to the social revolutionism of the interwar collectivity that went by the name Antifa in Palestine; and it is seen by some as having been born in the post-Second-World-War antifa committees of unoccupied Germany, such as the Antifaschistischer Volksausschuß of Dresden. But the direct work of piecing together in organized form the politics that in the twenty-first century is understood as antifa was done by the likes of Anti-Fascist Action and the Red Warriors and the others like them – the antifascist groups made c. 1985. Looking back many years later, a militant of the Red Warriors named Julien – one of the group's first members in 1985 – could boast with plausibility: "We were the first guys, here in Paris, to develop this radical and militant antifa activism in the streets."[144]

Though the Red Warriors and Anti-Fascist Action worked to turn the politics of antifascism in the same general direction, the two groups were far from identical to each other. Anti-Fascist Action, the London group, worked initially as a formal mass organization interested in staging well-choreographed events and establishing a sprawling network of chapters to coordinate action. By contrast, the Red Warriors, the Paris group, were a small and tightly knit informal collectivity of youths, all of whom knew each other face to face, who spent a lot of their time on the streets of the city and were fed up with the neo-Nazi skinheads who dominated the local street culture and who bullied, beat, and terrorized kids like them.

In the markets, in the grands boulevards, and on the métro, the Red Warriors hunted neo-Nazi skinheads. Their aim was to smash fascism at the point of origin, to win the streets and to make the price of fascism so high that the neo-Nazis of Paris would stay home or find something else to do or be. Skinhead culture had become big in Paris several years

---

[144] *Antifa: Chasseurs de skins* (dir. Marc-Aurèle Vecchione, 2008).

before – kids had started listening to the Oi! music of British punk bands such as Sham 69 and studying their look. Local bands started up. Concerts took on the fervor of religious revival meetings.

But by 1985 the skinhead culture in Paris, as elsewhere, had become dominated by the extreme right. Neo-Nazism, white power, and violent bigotry ruled the scene. The Front National, led by the race-baiting exclusionary nationalist Jean-Marie Le Pen, had just won over two million votes and was making appeals to the country's alienated youth typified by the punks and skinheads.

For Paxton, the grounding of late twentieth-century neo-Nazism in skinhead culture was a sign of the movement's alienation from politics in general and its lack of "authentic" fascism in particular. "The adolescent skinheads who flaunt the swastika today in parts of Europe," he writes in his 1998 essay, "seem so alien and marginal that they constitute a law-and-order problem (serious though that may be) rather than a recurrence of authentic mass-based fascism." This normative reading of skinhead neo-Nazism, offered from the perspective of legal authorities and unconvinced of the skinheads' ideological agency, makes for a sharp contrast to the lived perception of the Red Warriors and the rest of the era's skinhead antifa movement in Paris.

Paxton's assessment also diverges from the Red Warriors' perception in another way. Whereas for the Red Warriors the right-wing skinheads' Nazi performativity marked them as deeply, even fundamentally, fascist, for Paxton the transnationalism of skinhead neo-Nazism – its reliance, outside of Germany, on Nazi German aesthetics – demonstrated the movement's distance from actual fascism. A true "recurrence" of fascism, he argues, would be "astutely decked out in the patriotic emblems of their own countries." I just described skinhead neo-Nazism as performatively and aesthetically transnational, heavily dependent on borrowings from Nazi German culture, but Paxton's attention to nationalist iconography – "patriotic emblems" – makes me think that perhaps it's less telling to consider neo-Nazis' flaunting of the Iron Cross, the othala rune, the swastika, and other such emblems as signals of a transnationally appropriated culture; perhaps it's more telling to consider the neo-Nazis' use of these cultural emblems as signals communicating a narrow nationalism: white nationalism, as a form of alternative nationalism, as a project of rejecting Paxton's normative notion of "their own countries" and instead working toward a country of their own conjuring, "the white nation." To interpret matters thus, though, means interpreting skinhead neo-Nazism not as apolitical rowdyism (a problem of law and order) but rather as a collective project of popular politics. It also means investing movement iconography, emblems, symbols, and aesthetics with political significance. Paxton, though, cautions against this. Regarding the adolescent skinheads flaunting the swastika, he warns: "Focusing on external symbols, which are subject to superficial imitation, adds to confusion about what may legitimately be considered fascist."[145]

In Paris, as elsewhere in the mid-1980s, the neo-Nazi skinhead movement organized, recruited, and performed in cultural spaces more effectively than it did in spaces of formal politics. The neo-Nazi skinheads of Paris had their own musical bands and also showed up at the shows of others, ready to cause a row. Their aim always was to impose physical dominance over the gathering spaces of the Paris youth.

It was against this set of circumstances that the founders of the Red Warriors created the group, in a Paris squat called "L'U.S.I.N.E.," and started taking the fight to the fascists, often taking them by surprise in the streets. The Red Warriors also worked security for antifascist left-wing punk bands such as Bérurier Noir, who put on shows in L'U.S.I.N.E., cursed out the Front National and other Nazis from the stage, and always energetically communicated the band's central message to the youth of France: abandon the divisive identitarian politics of hatred promulgated by the fascists and, instead, embrace a multiracial generational unity – "get united to win" was a significant refrain of the band's music.

The Red Warriors played a leading role in what became a multicity movement of "redskins" – skinheads with left-wing (red) politics. The movement's participants took their nickname from a British punk band, the members of which were antifascists who had been in the Anti-Nazi League (the band had come together in 1982 after the collapse of an earlier iteration, a band named No Swastikas). Though influenced by such past antifascist efforts, the skinhead antifa politics taking form around 1985 – in France and beyond – was largely the work of a new – and still very young – generation. Just as the young had put together the freedom antifascism of the previous age, the antifa of the late twentieth and early twenty-first centuries has been a strikingly autonomous youth-driven politics. However, whereas freedom antifascism had located fascism in the social order imposed by much older antagonists, the front line of fascism for many of the early antifa skinheads were kids as young as they themselves were. In France, as elsewhere, skinhead antifa quickly broke fascism's stranglehold on the politics of youth street culture. The violent,

---

[145] Paxton, "Five Stages of Fascism," 3.

intense militancy of "redskin" groups such as the Red Warriors had the almost immediate effect of reducing the ranks of the fascist skinhead movement nationwide.

The Red Warriors also established connections with antifascism's larger formal organizations in France. The Red Warriors began working with SOS Racisme – a group created by socialists, which announced itself to a mass audience with a June 1985 music festival in the Place de la Concorde – and also began working with SCALP – the Section Carrément Anti Le Pen (the "Absolutely Anti-Le Pen Group"), which militant anarchists had put together spontaneously in the proudly antifascist city of Toulouse in 1984, amid the Front National's explosive growth that year. Both SOS Racisme and SCALP organized antifascist mass demonstrations, and SCALP also organized forceful direct actions to impede the Front National's attempts to hold rallies. For both SOS Racisme and SCALP, the Red Warriors provided solidarity and security.[146]

Akin to the Front National (FN) of France was the National Front (NF) of Britain that the Anti-Nazi League had opposed in the 1970s. The NF, though, had crumbled by that decade's end. In the early 1980s, as the historian of British antifascism Nigel Copsey has suggested, "the urgency that rallied mass opposition to the NF between 1977–9 disappeared." The Anti-Nazi League disbanded. But by 1985 some of that old urgency had returned. White supremacist violence had spiked in Britain's Black and Asian communities. An NF gang of skinheads had carried out an audacious assault on the band members of the Redskins while they were onstage at a festival in London.[147] Across Britain, nationalism and militarism were generating mass appeal; Thatcherism ruled. The NF may have crumbled, but among antifascists there was a feeling that they themselves had overly demobilized in response, that they had left the path open for a resurgence of the radical right. In July 1985, a meeting of 300 assorted antifascists declared "the need to build an anti-fascist front of groups willing to combat fascist activity in this country. We see the need to oppose racism and fascism physically, on the streets, and ideologically."[148] Their vehicle for doing so was to be Anti-Fascist Action.

---

[146] *Antifa; Scalp, 1984–1992: Comme un indien métropolitain: Aux origines du movement antifasciste radical* (Paris: No Pasaran, 2005); Gilles Vergnon, *L'antifascisme en France: De Mussolini à Le Pen* (Rennes: Presses universitaires de Rennes, 2009), 195–197; Jean-Paul Gautier, *Antifascisme(s): Des années 1960 à nos jours* (Paris: Éditions Syllepse, 2022), 128–148.

[147] Copsey, *Anti-Fascism in Britain*, 151, 158.

[148] Birchall, *Beating the Fascists*, 107.

The points of emphasis for the new organization were to throw up a big tent and yet also to remain militant. Anti-Fascist Action's first show of grit was Remembrance Sunday 1985. Set aside annually to commemorate the war dead, Remembrance Day in Britain and throughout the British Empire and Commonwealth has always been a day full of official liturgical ritual and dramatized spectacles of authority. But it has also always presented opportunities for popular political assertion. Remembrance Day's roots are in Armistice Day, the memorial day created in the aftermath of the First World War. From the beginning, fascists and antifascists have paid special attention to the day's symbolic powers. In the 1970s and early 1980s, the NF had staged marches to the Cenotaph war memorial in Whitehall on Remembrance Sunday. The marchers were known to wrap up their annual event by attacking the ongoing anti-apartheid picket outside the South African embassy.[149] By 1985, the NF treated its march as a matter of customary privilege, earned by precedent.

Anti-Fascist Action's earliest members sought to unsettle that. As was explained in *Searchlight*, in 1985, "It was not without some considerable degree of soul searching that anti-fascists decided this year that the National Front could no longer be allowed to parade unopposed on Remembrance Sunday." For the members of the new Anti-Fascist Action, the day's deeper meaning drew on memory of the Second World War more than that of the First. Remembrance Sunday, *Searchlight* argued, was the day for commemorating "the ultimate sacrifice made by so many millions" – with a number so large, the magazine was subtly marking Remembrance Sunday as more than a national day of memory, as a day, rather, belonging to all humanity. *Searchlight* also depicted the Second World War as having been a global fight against "nazism and fascism" – Remembrance Sunday, then, was not an apolitical day of nationwide common feeling (not a day of armistice in the ongoing ideological civil war), but rather a day of ideological recollection.[150] Anti-Fascist Action's turnout at the NF's point of assembly amounted to a declaration of antifascism's recomposition.

On the following year's Remembrance Sunday, Anti-Fascist Action held a mass demonstration meant to mark the day's memorial significance as specifically antifascist by laying a wreath of its own at the Cenotaph. Doing so wasn't a simple retort in kind to the fascists' act of wreath laying.

---

[149] An ex-Liverpool AFA member, *Anti-Fascist Action – An Anarchist Perspective* (London: Kate Sharpley Library, 2007), 7.
[150] "Never Again!" *Searchlight: The Anti-Fascist Monthly* 126 (Dec. 1985), 2.

And it was meant not only to complicate the nature of the memory being invoked in the act of remembrance (by placing emphasis on the Second World War and its ideological content), it was also meant to complicate the nature of the act of remembrance itself. Anti-Fascist Action accomplished this by explaining that the act of wreath laying had been done, as the group put it at the time, "in memory of the victims of fascist violence, yesterday and today" – such memory, that of both yesterday and today, did away with notions of memory as an act made in a self-contained post-historical present, carried out to reflect upon a separate and distinct historical past, a past that had ended.[151] By explaining the wreath laying thus, Anti-Fascist Action posed remembrance as a tying together of past and present. Such a strategy was reminiscent of the memorial politics practiced by Melbourne's Jewish antifascists in the aftermath of the Second World War or that promulgated by Beatriz Allende when she spoke on the anniversary of the Chilean coup and drew together notions of we-remember-the-dead and we-remember-to-fight. Anti-Fascist Action's act had the same logic: we remember, which is to say we remember to fight.

Anti-Fascist Action's successes in militant mass mobilization had transnational ramifications. Antifascist skinheads in the Twin Cities of Minnesota took the British group's example to heart when they set about organizing against local fascists in Minneapolis and St. Paul. In 1987, local white fascist youths had set off, as one local put it, "a mini race war" by jumping a Black teen. Neo-Nazi and white-power groups, such as the White Knights, had grown in the Twin Cities, recruiting among local skinheads. Skinhead culture, itself profoundly transnational, had not at all originated as a likely base for fascist organizing. The culture had originated in London in the 1960s by drawing together white working-class kids and young Black Jamaican locals familiar with Jamaica's "rude boy" culture and ska music. Skinhead culture took shape as an interracial, socially rebellious counterculture: unruly nonconformism and personal equality signified by shaved heads and Doc Martens boots. The fusion of punk and ska musics generated the Oi! music scene, which became a stage for skinhead culture's ongoing enactment. The skinheads in the Twin Cities who were determined to counter the likes of the White Knights belonged to a local multiracial clique known as the Baldies. After the "mini race war" was set off, they created Anti-Racist Action, the name of which they meant as an homage to Anti-Fascist Action. Anti-Racist Action engaged in physical direct action to deny the Nazi groups the

---

[151] Quotation from Birchall, *Beating the Fascists*, 121.

spaces they used to organize, demonstrate, and recruit. Anti-Racist Action itself grew into a transnational movement organization, with chapters in Toronto, Montréal, and smaller Canadian cities.[152]

Antifascist organizing took off among skinheads. In New York City, in 1987, skinheads organized themselves as SHARP – Skinheads Against Racial Prejudice. Like Anti-Racist Action, SHARP has operated as a network of locally empowered militant self-defense groups and has organized campaigns of direct action. Also like Anti-Racist Action, SHARP from the start has been multiracial. SHARPs have professed a street politics of antiracism, antifascism, and opposition to antisemitism. In the late 1980s, one group of SHARPs based in Los Angeles – most of them teenage boys and girls – constituted Black, white, Latino, and Asian members; among their main organizers was a Jewish skinhead in the Marines who wore a yellow armband, "with pride," he declared.[153] SHARP also became a transnational collectivity, with chapters in Montréal and Winnipeg, and then, thanks, at least in part, to the efforts of the Oi! band the Oppressed, SHARP began organizing in Britain, flipping the direction of influence among skinheads begun by Anti-Fascist Action. SHARP later grew more, taking root in Germany, the Czech Republic, Malaysia, and elsewhere.[154]

In the 1980s, antifa politics among the rebellious youths who were engaged in punk culture exploded in both East and West Germany. In West Germany, the greatest boom was in 1985, after the police in Frankfurt shot water cannons and killed the antifascist demonstrator Günter Sare during a protest against neo-Nazis. In East Germany, the spark for mass antifa politics flashed two years later when neo-Nazi skinheads staged an assault on a punk concert in East Berlin, at the leftist venue Zionskirche. Within weeks, Antifa Potsdam was postering; other groups soon followed.[155] Their efforts were guided by the rigorous and critical reporting of *Antifaschistisches Infoblatt*, published in Berlin beginning in 1987. The early *Antifa-Info* reported on everything from the violence of "Nazi-Skins" in Dresden to "the antifascist resistance" of the Antifa-Jugend-Front

---

[152] Shannon Clay et al., *We Go Where They Go: The Story of Anti-Racist Action* (Oakland: PM Press, 2023), 22.

[153] David Haldane, "Gathering of Anti-Racist Skinheads Belies the Neo-Nazi Image," *Los Angeles Times*, July 31, 1989, part II, p. 10. On Antifa in the United States, see Bray, *Antifa*; Stanislav Vysotsky, *American Antifa: The Tactics, Culture, and Practice of Militant Antifascism* (Abingdon: Routledge, 2021).

[154] Timothy S. Brown, "Subcultures, Pop Music and Politics: Skinheads and 'Nazi Rock' in England and Germany," *Journal of Social History* 38, no. 1 (Fall 2004), 157–178.

[155] Christin Jänicke, "The Invisible 'Antifa-Ost': The Struggles of Anti-Hegemonic Engagement in East Germany," *Partecipazione e conflitto* 17, no. 1 (2024), 64–79.

(Antifa Youth Front) in Leipzig (the first AJF had been organized in 1986 by Antifa-Westberlin).[156] The magazine's brilliant reworking of the old Antifaschistische Aktion emblem (making one of the two flags black) is only one example of the magazine's record of vivid and effortlessly stylish iconography.[157]

Keeping true to the DIY ethos of punk culture, SHARP's expanded transnational presence has been driven by locals – somewhere, wherever – deciding, autonomously, to call themselves SHARPs. Skinheads all over have done this, pulling antifa politics into their local scenes and freely making it their own. One of the more dynamic and enduring examples of SHARP's antifa politics is that of Buenos Aires. There, the SHARP playbook of antifa politics has had the usual effect, locally, of pulling together different parts of the skinhead scene and giving them a unifying framework for working through their various problems. The stress that the first antifa skinheads in Buenos Aires put on unity, performing it into a lived reality, has stuck with the movement through the decades and is a reason that the antifa movement in Buenos Aires has remained active and militant.

The history of the movement has played out in three acts over three decades: the movement's ignition, set off by the fanzine *Golpe Justo* in the 1990s; the community-based radicalism of the group Acción Antifascista, begun in the 2000s; and the prefigurative performances of freedom within the Club Social y Deportiva La Cultura del Barrio, initiated in the 2010s.

In the 1980s and early 1990s, the city's skinhead scene had been, at least in part and overwhelmingly in the way it was perceived, ultra-rightist. Bands and fans had connections to neo-Nazi groups such as the Movimiento Nacional Socialista ("National Socialist Movement") and the Partido Nacionalista de los Trabajadores ("National Socialist Workers' Party"). Local skinheads were reading the writings of Hitler as well as those of the antisemitic Argentinian neo-Nazi named Federico Rivanera Carlés, author of *Los Judíos son nuestros enemigos!* ("The Jews are our enemies!"). Rivanera Carlés had once been jailed on charges of plotting a coup d'état and was the guiding force of the Movimiento Nacional Socialista and its organ, the *Ataque* (the "Attack," like the Nazi propagandist Joseph Goebbels's newspaper, the *Angriff*). In the 1980s, the Movimiento

---

[156] "Dresden – neue Hauptstadt der »Nazi-Bewegung«?" and "Antifaschistischer Widerstand Leipzig," *Antifaschistisches Infoblatt*, no. 14 (Spring 1991), 22–28; Bernd Langer, *Antifaschistische Aktion: Geschichte einer linksradikalen Bewegung* (Münster: Unrast, 2014), 206.

[157] For examples of the reworked emblem, see *Antifaschistisches Infoblatt*, nos. 6/7 (Feb. 1989), 2; *Antifaschistisches Infoblatt*, no. 16 (Winter 1991), 57.

Nacional Socialista had ties to the Argentine skinhead scene through the band Comando Suicida (named in homage to the Argentine Army from the era of the military junta's rule).[158]

For some local skinheads, though, the fascists didn't define the scene. That was the stance of young Juan Carlos Varela, who knew skinhead culture and Oi! and ska music inside and out and put an almost mystical faith in their liberatory implications. He wanted to put those implications into practice and also to reclaim Buenos Aires's skinhead culture from the fascists. Doing so, he wrote, would mean reclaiming what it had meant "to be part of the skinhead scene in the years '67–69," when London's working-class white kids and young Jamaican immigrants, "called Rude Boys," first made the scene. "That's why," Varela insisted, "it's clear that the skinheads' origin is MULTIRACIAL AND MULTICULTURAL." He accepted that skinhead culture had lost its way since then – "a negative epoch," he wrote, had arisen in the late 1970s and had continued through the 1980s – but he also insisted that there was still much in the culture that was antithetical to fascism and that could be pulled forth to defeat it.[159] Varela didn't accept the portrayal of the skinheads in the news as nothing but Nazis. His read of the situation was closer to that of another local who was part of the scene, Helmostro Punk, who had once written that Buenos Aires was "on the verge of a punk civil war" between street-fighting leftist anarchists and the scene's "fachos" (slang for "fascists") who hailed the Nazi cult hero Rudolf Hess at their concerts, subscribed to the neo-fascist Third Position ideology, and followed Comando Suicida.[160]

The antifascist skinhead scene in Buenos Aires began in 1995 when Varela started publishing his own DIY fanzine, which he named *Golpe Justo*. He wrote with an infectious love of Oi! and ska, and he also, from the first issue onward, called forth a politics of skinhead antifascism.

---

[158] Alfred S. Hopkins, "Right-wing Bands Still Active in Argentina," *Latinamerica Press* 19, no. 10 (Mar. 19, 1987), 7; Horacio Verbitsky, "Reflexiones para evitar otra derrota," *Fin de siglo* (Aug. 1987), 39; Matías Gatica, *La cultura skinhead antifascista: De Jamaica a Buenos Aires* (Liniers, Buenos Aires: Corazón de Perrx Editorial, 2019), 155; Federico Rivanera Carlés, *Los judíos son nuestros enemigos!* (Buenos Aires: Instituto de Investigaciones sobre la Cuestión Judía, 1987); Federico Rivanera Carlés, "¿Un estado judío en Argentina?" *Ataque*, Oct. 13, 1986, p. 1. See also Federico Rivanera Carlés, *El judaísmo y la semana trágica: La verdadera historia de los sucesos de enero de 1919* (Buenos Aires: Instituto de Investigaciones sobre la Cuestión Judía, 1986). Rivanera Carlés is a descendant of Manuel Carlés, on whom see Sandra McGee Deutsch, *Counterrevolution in Argentina, 1900–1932: The Argentine Patriotic League* (Lincoln: University of Nebraska Press, 1986).

[159] *Golpe Justo* 1 (Jan. 1996), 3, 5.

[160] Helmostro Punk [Mauri Kurcbard], "Guerra civil punkoide," *Fin de siglo* (Oct. 1987), 41.

He wrote that he wanted "to improve the image of a scene that is very distorted thanks to the fascism of a few and that is harmful to many."[161]

Varela wanted to counter both skinhead fascism itself and the larger society that was so quick to accept the image of all skinheads as fascists. He set out to do so with a militant skinhead antifascism rooted in the ideas at the core of the music. He declared, "The voice of Oi! is calling us with its message for all the true skinheads, punxs, rude boys, hardcore kids, and straights. The voice of Oi! is Unity." As if to explain the name of his fanzine, he declared, "the golpe in the streets is yours and mine, UNITED AGAINST SOCIETY!" Varela always insisted that his aim was to reclaim the emancipatory impulses at work in skinhead culture's genesis. "We must remember," he wrote, "the true spirit of Oi!" Explaining, he exhorted: "True Oi! is against racism and fascism." Using the fanzine as his megaphone, Varela organized a Buenos Aires chapter of SHARP, "to terminate fascism, Nazism, racism, and discrimination of whatever type, and thus to reclaim the original spirit of the skinheads."[162]

Starting from one fanzine, the antifa movement of Buenos Aires quickly outgrew even the SHARP chapter that Varela had organized in the fanzine's pages. In 2001, local antifascists established Acción Antifascista. The group's early literature described it as totally committed to "the antifascist struggle and all of the ramifications of that struggle." Decisions were made by assemblies, "without leaders, without hierarchies of any type."[163] Acción Antifascista took off by taking part in the nationwide mass disobedience movement of 2001 and 2002 fueled by popular anger toward the International Monetary Fund's decision to impose austerity on Argentina at a moment when its economy was acutely vulnerable. Unemployment and underemployment exploded. Outraged demonstrators created roadblocks and occupied buildings. Unemployed workers took direct action by claiming shuttered places of business and running them collectively. Acción Antifascista contributed to the mass direct action in Avellaneda, an industrial port city in Gran Buenos Aires that became symbolic of the entire anti-IMF movement after the police in the city engaged in mass arrests and murdered two protesters in June 2002. In Avellaneda, Antifascista Acción set up a cultural center in an occupied building and helped to create soup kitchens and a workers' cooperative. On March 24, 2008, Acción Antifascista held its first "festival

---

[161] *Golpe Justo* 1 (Jan. 1996), 3–5.
[162] *Golpe Justo* 1 (Jan. 1996), 3–5, 21.
[163] *Acción antifascista Bs. As: Boletín informativo* 1, no. 2 (Winter 2002), 2.

antifascista," or "festi antifa," in the streets. Fascists still commemorate March 23 as the anniversary of the 1919 meeting in the Piazza San Sepolcro of Milan at which Benito Mussolini supposedly created fascism. An antifascist mobilization held one day after the March 23 anniversary carried a clear antifascist message – a message that had been consistently at the core of antifascism since its origin – that fascism has to be fought from its inception. Acción Antifascista soon held more street festivals. As one member explained, "With Acción Antifascista, we had a need to win the streets." The fifth festi antifa, held by Acción Antifascista, again on March 24, one year after the first to the day, was violently broken up by the police. Acción Antifascista still kept holding street festivals but also started to think about establishing a secure home base – as the same member put it, "a place of our own."[164]

The solution was the Club Social y Deportiva La Cultura del Barrio, known as LCDB. Established in 2011 in the neighborhood of Villa Crespo, LCDB was to become, as Acción Antifascista literature put it, a place "free from wrongheaded prejudices that still afflict us." LCDB's mission is thus to serve as a place "free of discrimination, without chauvinism or xenophobia," a place animated instead by "camaraderie, mutual respect, and solidarity." LCDB is for everyone ("todxs"), though its literature stresses its origin in skinhead culture – more specifically, its origin in the "cultural battle" to reclaim "the true values of this culture," rather than what is written about it in the press. The club's literature states: "Let's be clear: skinhead is not fascism!"[165] Such rhetoric has much of the spirit of Juan Carlos Varela's DIY fanzine from the '90s about it. If ever there was a movement that has stayed true to its roots, it is skinhead antifa Buenos Aires. LCDB keeps, as well, a commitment to Varela's obsessive dream of the unified scene. One of the club's recurrent events has been a "festi skin," or "festival of antifascist skinhead culture," that the club has named "If the Kids Are United" – with the name written and spoken in English, in homage to the ferocious and foundational 1978 Oi! song of that same title, by Sham 69. For antifa Buenos Aires, the message remains the music. At an "If the Kids Are United" in 2019, one of the skinheads from the scene, the singer Checho Scarponi, performed with his band in front of a banner with the antifascist three arrows (a symbol first created in 1932 in Weimar Germany), underneath the two-flag emblem of Antifaschistische Aktion (also, of course, from Weimar Germany), with one of the two

---

[164] Gatica, *Cultura skinhead antifascista*, 166, 168.
[165] Gatica, *Cultura skinhead antifascista*, 169–170.

flags black (as reworked by *Antifa-Info* in the 1980s). In short, a long and transnational antifascist history was at work in the performance onstage.

Skinhead antifa has cut similar paths elsewhere. In São Paulo, SHARPs are part of a punk scene that turned antifa in synch with Varela's efforts in Buenos Aires. Neo-Nazi skinheads threatened to dominate local youth culture in the municipality of São Paulo and the broader metropolitan area's "ABC municipalities" (Santo André, São Bernardo do Campo, and São Caetano do Sul). White-power skinheads attacked a radio station in 1992; the following year a group of thirty neo-Nazi skinheads in Santo André murdered a Black student named Fábio dos Santos. So in 1994 punks took part in organizing antifascist demonstrations. After members of the Carecas do ABC (a fascist skinhead group modeled on the integralista greenshirt organization that Plínio Salgado had founded back in 1932) beat to death a gay man named Edson Neris in 2000, local antifascist punks in response organized the "Jornada Antifascista," which became an annual event in São Paulo.[166]

Throughout the antifa age, antifascists have tried to counter-organize against the new radical right. In Japan, the "Noriko Calderon Incident" of April 11, 2009, provoked a wave of antifascist organizing. The incident took place in Warabi, a dense working-class city north of Tokyo. Zaitokukai, a right-wing ultranationalist group created two years earlier, marched in the city's streets to protest the presence of Noriko Calderon, a local Filipina girl in junior high. Calderon's parents had been deported after their visas had expired, but Japanese authorities had allowed Calderon to stay longer. Zaitokukai marched on both her school and her home in Warabi. Zaitokukai had organized similar protests in the recent past; this time, though, they faced counterdemonstrators in force for the first time. The group Giakokujin Haijodemo ni Hantaisurukai (Association to Oppose Xenophobic Demonstrations) had organized the counterdemonstration, which ended up including direct-action methods to stop Zaitokukai.[167] More efforts to stop Zaitokukai followed, and soon a movement had taken shape. Noma Yasumichi, the founder of the antifascist direct-action group known as the Counter-Racist Action Collective, or CRAC, suggests that it was early in the next decade that activists began to conceptualize themselves as comprising "an antifascism movement." More specific than antifascism,

---

[166] "O Movimento Anarco-Punk e a luta antifascista no Brasil," in *Antifa: Modo de usar*, ed. Acácio Augusto (Rio de Janeiro: Hedra, 2020), 25–31.

[167] Daiki Shibuichi, "The Struggle Against Hate Groups in Japan: The Invisible Civil Society, Leftist Elites and Anti-Racism Groups," *Social Science Japan Journal* 19, no. 1 (Winter 2016), 74.

though, activists dramatized their movement as antifa. They drew on punk music and street fashion to draw together an ideologically unlikely protest coalition. Antifa was their glue. It was ironic that it would be so: early on, activists willing to demonstrate against racism, exclusionary nationalism, neoliberal institutions, and the repressive national government were wary of the label. Noma himself was reluctant because he thought the word gave the impression that "we are extreme left or anarchists with black flags." With time, though, antifa became a unifying identity. The movement became more and more explicitly antifascist. After a 2013 right-wing rally in Osaka that featured an orator calling for the "genocide" of a Korean community, a direct-action antifa group named Shibakitai came together to defend Korean residents whenever Zaitokukai marched on their neighborhoods. Shibakitai adopted the classic antifascist slogan of the Spanish Civil War era as its mantra: "¡No pasarán!"[168]

It was a fitting reminder that antifascism's history, ongoing, is open and embedded within a context wider than any one national society and deeper, as well, than any one age.

Conclusion: Staging and Aging Antifascist and Fascist Histories

LCDB, the antifa social center in the heart of Buenos Aires, isn't that far from where the antifascist women of the Junta de la Victoria knitted sweaters for Allied troops during the Second World War. (For that matter, neither is it all that far from the building that had housed the Italian mutual aid society where antifascisti had exchanged gunfire with fascisti way back in 1923.) Beyond that geographical proximity, though, the differences between the antifa skinheads and the antifascist sweater-knitters stand out more than their similarities. A history that seals the two groups within a single unfolding national tradition of Argentine antifascism wouldn't explain either one very well. Similarly, a scheme that imagines the Junta de la Victoria as representative of an early "stage" of a national antifascism and LCDB as representative of a late "stage" wouldn't explain much about either one's place in history. LCDB has belonged, first and foremost, to its age of global antifascist history – it belongs to the transnational currents of skinhead antifa, Oi! unity, and DIY social revolutionism distinct to the antifa age. The Junta de la Victoria, likewise, belonged very much to its own age, the age of total war waged between global democracy

---

[168] Vivian Shaw, "Strategies of Ambivalence: Cultures of Liberal Antifa in Japan," *Radical History Review*, no. 138 (Oct. 2020), 147, 151, 154.

and global fascism, an age of deep transnational solidarity and antifascist commitment to aiding the Allies – and to converting the Allies' campaign into an antifascist war for, in the words of Nehru, "true freedom everywhere."

This essay has been an attempt to work through a methodological claim about the problems of the "stagist" historical method and the whole of developmentalist social thought that underpins such a method. The claim is based on a critique of historical thinking that spatially walls off one national society from another and that temporally seals a nation's history within its own internal chronos, unfolding from its own Year One, a chronological start point conceived of as undisturbed by any embeddedness within a wider context of transnational and global history.

I chose Robert Paxton's classic essay "The Five Stages of Fascism" as my subject of critique, I should stress, because it is exemplary. It is so in a double sense of the word: Paxton's essay is exemplary in that it stands out as a praiseworthy model, an example of the best of scholarly works animated by its kind of thought; and it is exemplary in that it is an extreme example of its school of thought, the social developmentalist school epitomized by modernization theory. It's hard to imagine a purer example of what I've called "stagist" history than "The Five Stages of Fascism." As regards fascism, Paxton's stagist historical consciousness and the distinctive "comparison as a way of thinking" that it prompts work together to produce a peculiar mix of quietism and anxiety. They conjure a present radically divided from the past. And they situate fascism as having lived squarely in the past – particularly in German and Italian pasts, and more generally in a European past. And yet its ghost lurks always near, threatening a return. Situated thus, fascism takes on the feel of something with enough potentiality of repetition to be anxious about and yet also paradoxically impossible to realize in the singular present, making antifascist mobilization anachronistic. Such an understanding of the present, based on comparisons to the past – with each understood, because of the rules of analogy, as disconnected from the other, distinct so as to constitute separate subjects that might be profitably compared against each other – mystifies the present by alienating it from the past. Such a way of thinking, again, ought to be fought against and vanquished. However, for any reader skeptical of the piety that criticism is a higher form of praise, it's worth bringing up once more that Paxton's essay remains a splendid work of scholarship with which to think through the question of fascism's nature. Even as I've critiqued the essay's stagism, I happily concede that Paxton has fashioned wonderfully generative ideas of "mobilizing passions" and has worked out penetrating claims regarding the powers of political practice to signify deep undercurrents of political thought often – in particular in the case of fascists – quite purposefully left unspoken.

What have been antifascism's mobilizing passions? Its signifying practices? Throughout its ages, antifascism has been a politics mobilized by, obviously, passionate opposition to (what the antifascists interpret to be) fascism. Solidarity, collective self-defense, direct action, physical confrontation, the struggle over specific space in which to express one's politics, the idealization of unity, and the mourning of martyrs – these have been constants of antifascist history. Because these constants came about and have been sustained in the context of the antifascists' engagement with fascists, it makes sense that a list of fascism's constants might include a mix of similar and directly inverse commitments (and so indeed does Paxton's list of fascism's mobilizing passions include just such a mix). The constancy of the antifascist commitments I've listed doesn't mean, though, that they amount to an antifascist minimum or antifascism's necessary elements. Social revolutionism, anticolonialism and anti-imperialism, the veneration of resistance, memorial contestation, anti-genocidal consciousness, the pursuit of freedom and liberation, communing, antiracism, cultural rebellion, and autonomy – antifascists have worked out commitments to such things bit by bit, over time, as they've gone about their struggle through the ages.

My use of ages has been, to an extent, instrumental, useful for constructing a counterhistory, or a history that is, at least as I see it, useful for throwing a light on certain flaws of the received story. That, of course, doesn't mean that the counterhistory necessarily stands up as the proper telling worth putting one's faith in. The extent to which it's useful to conceptualize the history of a political form such as antifascism by ages is a separate matter from that of whether it's unuseful to conceptualize one by stages. It's also a matter best left, at this point, in the hands of the reader. To that end, I ask you to remember that perhaps the broadest aim of this work has been to put forth a history of antifascism so as to offer you some tools and materials for constructing, in your head, an understanding of your own – of fascism's history. Historians know well that the history of fascism is a devilishly difficult thing to comprehend. My wager with this work is that the praxis of the Arditi del Popolo – and the Jewish Council to Combat Fascism and Anti-Semitism and the Black Panthers and the Comité Chileno de Solidaridad con la Resistencia Antifascista and the SHARPs and all the various collectivities that have gone by the name Antifa – is useful for "thinking along with" as you critically sort through the different ways to make sense of fascism's history and the different ways to put fascism in history.

In closing, I'd like to take up the idea of antifascist history's, and fascist history's, "aging." By this, I mean not only to suggest the act of organizing antifascism's, or fascism's, history into a number of ages but also to suggest that by the twenty-first century the histories of antifascism and fascism, like those of the other grand and universalized isms of modernity, have gotten a bit long. By the time of this Element's writing, fascism and antifascism have both entered their second centuries. For all their dramatic changes and contestations through the ages, neither has developed to what you might call a higher stage. But neither has either of them remained in its original form: There *have* been shifts and breaks. Also, it's worth considering the likelihood that neither fascism nor antifascism is near its end. New ages will be made. More struggles will be waged.

And those struggles will draw on the ever-longer and ever-more-entangled histories of fascism and antifascism. I've already suggested that LCDB captures much about the globally shared antifa ethos of its age – the punk, ska, and Oi!, the skinheads on the floor, and the ongoing legacy of SHARP. But it not only absorbs the spatially wider transnational history of its age. It also incorporates the temporally longer transnational history of antifascism. Consider the three-arrow iconography and the two-flag (black-and-red) emblem labeled "Antifaschistische Aktion" that were onstage for the 2019 "If the Kids Are United" festi skin. By this point in the twenty-first century, the symbols and markers of antifascism are drawn forth from a deep well. People today and tomorrow who choose to draw upon antifascism's history in acting out their own politics do not, and will not, reenact or mimic or reproduce or restage acts of the past. They don't need to worry about the authenticity or the legitimacy of their politics. Neither do they, or will they, start from scratch, from Year One of Stage One. Rather, they are likely to begin armed with some knowledge of this deep history.

Histories are resources, some of them quite valuable. They should be drawn upon, they should be taken up and offered anew. Do that and you make them new. And you also equip yourself to make a history of your own, even as you draw yourself into a larger history. What, I wonder, will be the name of antifascism's next age?

Bibliography

Acción antifascista Bs. As: Boletín informativo 1, no. 2 (Winter 2002).
"Actividades de solidaridad con la lucha del pueblo de Chile como parle de la gran jornada internacional." *Granma.* Sept. 7, 1974, p. 1.
African XYZ. "Afro Readers Say." *Baltimore Afro-American.* Aug. 18, 1934, p. 4.
Afro Correspondent. "'Respectable' Organizations Snub N.Y.'s Biggest Turn-out." *Baltimore Afro-American.* Aug. 10, 1935, p. 7.
Allende, Beatriz. *"... Before the Eyes and Conscience of the World": Beatriz Allende Speaks to the North American People.* New York: Venceremos Brigade, 1974.
"Un'altra giornata di conflitti con morti e feriti a Roma." *Stampa.* Nov. 11, 1921, p. 1.
Anderson, Benedict. *Imagined Communities: Reflections on the Origin and Spread of Nationalism.* London: Verso, 1991.
"Antifa" Palestine. *Les Troubles Sanglantes en Palestine 1936.* Brussels: Imprimerie Polyglotte, 1936.
Antifaschistisches Infoblatt, nos. 6/7 (Feb. 1989).
Antifaschistisches Infoblatt, no. 16 (Winter 1991).
"Antifaschistische Junge Garde in Berlin gegründet." *Rote Fahne.* July 21, 1929, p. 12.
"Antifaschistischer Widerstand Leipzig." *Antifaschistisches Infoblatt,* no. 14 (Spring 1991): 26–28.
"Antifascismo pratico." *Martello.* Mar. 31, 1923, p. 4.
Anti-Fascist Bulletin, no. 5 (Mar. 1971).
Argenteri, Letizia. *Tina Modotti: Between Art and Revolution.* New Haven: Yale University Press, 2003.
Barroso, Gustavo. *Os protocolos dos sábios de* Sião, third edition. 1936. Porto Alegre: Revisão, 1989.
Batinić, Jelena. *Women and Yugoslav Partisans: A History of World War II Resistance.* New York: Cambridge University Press, 2015.
Baumann, Gerold Gino. *Los voluntarios latinoamericanos en la guerra civil Española.* Cuenca: Ediciones de la Universidad de Castilla-La Mancha, 2009.
Bečka, Jan. *The National Liberation Movement in Burma during the Japanese Occupation Period (1941–1945).* Prague: Oriental Institute in Academia, 1983.

Beckman, Morris. *The 43 Group*. London: Centerprise, 1992.
"Berlin Permits Demonstration." *New York Times.* Aug. 2, 1929, p. 5.
Birchall, Sean. *Beating the Fascists: The Untold Story of Anti-Fascist Action*. London: Freedom Press, 2010.
"The Black Panther Party Calls for a United Front Against Fascism." *Black Panther*. June 28, 1969, p. 20.
Bloom, Joshua, and Waldo E. Martin, Jr. *Black Against Empire: The History and Politics of the Black Panther Party*. Oakland: University of California Press, 2013.
Braskén, Kasper. "Making Anti-Fascism Transnational: The Origins of Communist and Socialist Articulations of Resistance in Europe, 1923–1924." *Contemporary European History* 25, no. 4 (Nov. 2016): 573–596.
Braskén, Kasper. "'Make Scandinavia a Bulwark Against Fascism!' Hitler's Seizure of Power and the Transnational Anti-fascist Movement in the Nordic Countries." In *Anti-fascism in a Global Perspective: Transnational Networks, Exile Communities, and Radical Internationalism*, ed. Kasper Braskén, Nigel Copsey, and David J. Featherstone. Abingdon: Routledge, 2021.
Braskén, Kasper, Nigel Copsey, and David J. Featherstone, editors. *Anti-Fascism in a Global Perspective: Transnational Networks, Exile Communities, and Radical Internationalism*. Abingdon: Routledge, 2021.
"Braunes Hemd – blaues Hemd," *Berlin Volks-Zeitung*. Oct. 22, 1930, p. 3.
Bray, Mark. *Antifa: The Anti-Fascist Handbook*. Brooklyn: Melville House, 2017.
"Brothers in New York State Concentration Camp Form the Jonathan P. Jackson Commune." *Black Panther*. Jan. 9, 1971, p. 8.
Brown, Timothy S. "Subcultures, Pop Music and Politics: Skinheads and 'Nazi Rock' in England and Germany." *Journal of Social History* 38, no. 1 (Fall 2004): 157–178.
Buchanan, Tom. "'Shanghai-Madrid Axis'? Comparing British Responses to the Conflicts in Spain and China, 1936–39." *Contemporary European History* 21, no. 4 (Nov. 2012): 533–552.
Buchanan, Tom. "'The Dark Millions in the Colonies are Unavenged': Anti-Fascism and Anti-Imperialism in the 1930s." *Contemporary European History* 25, no. 4 (Nov. 2016): 645–665.
Campbell, Ian. *The Addis Ababa Massacre: Italy's National Shame*. Oxford: Oxford University Press, 2017.

"Celebran numerosas actividades en todo el mundo en solidaridad con la lucha del pueblo chileno contra el fascismo." *Granma*. Sept. 12, 1974, p. 1.

Cerda, Hernan Lavin. "Brasil, repression y tortura." *Punto Final*. June 22, 1971, p. 22.

Christiaens, Kim. "European Reconfigurations of Transnational Activism: Solidarity and Human Rights Campaigns on Behalf of Chile during the 1970s and 1980s." *International Review of Social History* 63, no. 3 (Dec. 2018): 413–448.

Ciccotti, Francesco. "La dittatura della menzogna." *Stampa*. Aug. 27, 1919, p. 1.

Clay, Shannon, Kristin Schwartz Lady, and Michael Staudenmaier. *We Go Where They Go: The Story of Anti-Racist Action*. Oakland: PM Press, 2023.

Cleaver, Kathleen. "Racism, Fascism, and Political Murder." *Black Panther*. Sept. 14, 1968, p. 8.

"Come parla il rinnegato Mussolini." *Martello*. June 15, 1920, p. 9.

"Commentary." *Sechaba* (Jan. 1967): 1, 16.

Conrad, Sebastian. *What Is Global History?* Princeton: Princeton University Press, 2016.

"Contro il fascismo." *Martello*. Oct. 7, 1922, p. 3.

Copsey, Nigel. *Anti-Fascism in Britain*, second edition. London: Routledge, 2017.

Courtois, Stéphane, Denis Peschanski, and Adam Rayski. *Le sang de l'étranger: les immigrés de la MOI dans la Résistance*. Paris: Fayard, 1989.

"Cronaca di Arezzo." *Avanti!* Sept. 25, 1921, p. 5.

Davenport-Hines, Richard. "Hay, Josslyn Victor, twenty-second earl of Erroll." In *Oxford Dictionary of National Biography Online*. Oxford: Oxford University Press, 2004.

Deutsch, Sandra McGee. *Counterrevolution in Argentina, 1900–1932: The Argentine Patriotic League*. Lincoln: University of Nebraska Press, 1986.

Deutsch, Sandra McGee. *Las Derechas: The Extreme Right in Argentina, Brazil, and Chile, 1890–1939*. Stanford: Stanford University Press, 1999.

Deutsch, Sandra McGee. *Gendering Antifascism: Women's Activism in Argentina and the World, 1918–1947*. Pittsburgh: University of Pittsburgh Press, 2023.

Diamant, David. *Combattants juifs dans l'armée républicaine espagnole*. Paris: Éditions Renouveau, 1979.

"Does Fascism Rule South Africa? Here Are a Few Facts!" *Spotlight on Africa* 11, no. 2 (Feb. 25, 1952): 2.

"Dresden – neue Hauptstadt der »Nazi-Bewegung«?" *Antifaschistisches Infoblatt*, no. 14 (Spring 1991): 22–25.

"Earl of Erroll As Blackshirt Delegate To Kenya." *Blackshirt*. June 29, 1934, p. 10.

Edelman, Marek. *The Ghetto Fights*. London: Bookmarks, 1990.

"Der Eid der 'Antifa.'" *Berliner Börsen-Zeitung*. Nov. 19, 1930, p. 3.

"Der einzig gerechte Krieg ist der Bürgerkrieg." *Berliner Börsen-Zeitung*. Aug. 2, 1929, p. 3.

Elkins, Caroline. *Imperial Reckoning: The Untold Story of Britain's Gulag in Kenya*. New York: Henry Holt, 2005.

An ex-Liverpool AFA Member. *Anti-Fascist Action – An Anarchist Perspective*. London: Kate Sharpley Library, 2007.

"Il fascismo e la lotta agraria in Puglia." *Avanti!* Feb. 12, 1921, p. 4.

Finchelstein, Federico. *From Fascism to Populism in History*. Oakland: University of California Press, 2017.

"La formidabile insurrezione della Puglia rossa contro la violenza fascista." *Avanti!* Feb. 26, 1921, p. 1.

"Le fortune del fascismo." *Stampa*. Jan. 30, 1921, p. 1.

Fronczak, Joseph. *Everything Is Possible: Antifascism and the Left in the Age of Fascism*. New Haven: Yale University Press, 2023.

Gatica, Matías. *La cultura skinhead antifascista: De Jamaica a Buenos Aires*. Liniers, Buenos Aires: Corazón de Perrx Editorial, 2019.

Gautier, Jean-Paul. *Antifascisme(s): Des années 1960 à nos jours*. Paris: Éditions Syllepse, 2022.

Gilbert, Shirli. *Music in the Holocaust: Confronting Life in the Nazi Ghettos and Camps*. Oxford, Eng.: Clarendon Press, 2005.

Gildea, Robert. *Fighters in the Shadows: A New History of the French Resistance*. Cambridge: Belknap Press, 2015.

Gilroy, Paul. *There Ain't No Black in the Union Jack: The Cultural Politics of Race and Nation*. 1987; Milton Park, Abingdon: Routledge, 2002.

Gluckstein, Donny. *A People's History of the Second World War: Resistance versus Empire*. London: Pluto, 2012.

"Golpe fascista: Última advertencia." *Rebelde* (Aug. 28, 1971): 11.

Golpe Justo 1 (Jan. 1996).

Goshal, Kumar. "As An Indian Sees It." *Pittsburgh Courier*. Nov. 14, 1942, p. 7.

Goswami, Manu. *Producing India: From Colonial Economy to National Space*. Chicago: University of Chicago Press, 2004.

"Il Governo per l'ordine pubblico." *Stampa*. Nov. 12, 1921, p. 1.

Grover, Warren. *Nazis in Newark*. New Brunswick: Transaction, 2003.

Gutman, Israel. *Resistance: The Warsaw Ghetto Uprising*. Boston: Houghton Mifflin, 1994.

Gutman, Yisrael. *The Jews of Warsaw, 1939–1943: Ghetto, Underground, Revolt*, trans. Ina Friedman. Bloomington: Indiana University Press, 1982.

H., R. D. "As to the Fascisti." *New York Times*. Dec. 5, 1922, p. 18.

Haldane, David. "Gathering of Anti-Racist Skinheads Belies the Neo-Nazi Image." *Los Angeles Times*. July 31, 1989, part II, p. 10.

Hardt, Michael. *The Subversive Seventies*. New York: Oxford University Press, 2023.

Harmer, Tanya. *Beatriz Allende: A Revolutionary Life in Cold War Latin America*. Chapel Hill: University of North Carolina Press, 2020.

The Highest Example of Heroism. Havana: Instituto Cubano del Libro, 1973.

Hobsbawm, Eric. *The Age of Extremes: A History of the World, 1914–1991*. 1994; New York: Vintage, 1996.

Hopkins, Alfred S. "Right-wing Bands Still Active in Argentina." *Latinamerica Press* 19, no. 10 (Mar. 19, 1987): 7.

Hughes, Langston. "Harlem Ball Player Now Captain in Spain." *Baltimore Afro-American*. Feb. 12, 1938, p. 6.

Hyslop, Jonathan, Kasper Braskén, and Neil Roos, editors. "Anti-Fascism in Southern Africa." Special Issue. *South African Historical Journal* 74, no. 1 (2022).

Ibárruri, Dolores. *En la lucha: Palabras y hechos, 1936–1939*. Moscow: Editorial Progreso, 1968.

"In Memory of Matteotti." *Nation* (June 2, 1926): 618–619.

"International Actions in Support of Abyssinia." *Negro Worker* (Sept. 1935): 12–14.

Jänicke, Christin. "The Invisible 'Antifa-Ost': The Struggles of Anti-Hegemonic Engagement in East Germany." *Partecipazione e conflitto* 17, no. 1 (2024): 64–79.

Kaiser, Max. *Jewish Antifascism and the False Promise of Settler Colonialism*. Cham, Switzerland: Palgrave Macmillan, 2022.

"Kenya: The Settlers' Case." *Round Table* 26, no. 101 (Dec. 1935): 82–97.

Kranj, Gregor. "Collaboration, Resistance and Liberation in the Balkans, 1941–1945." In *The Cambridge History of the Second World War*, vol. 2: *Politics and Ideology*, ed. Richard J. B. Bosworth and Joseph Maiolo. Cambridge: Cambridge University Press, 2015.

Langer, Bernd. *Antifaschistische Aktion: Geschichte einer linksradikalen Bewegung*. Münster: Unrast, 2014.

Latham, Michael E. *Modernization as Ideology: American Social Science and "Nation Building in the Kennedy Era*. Chapel Hill: University of North Carolina Press, 2000.

Leonhard, Wolfgang. *Die Revolution entläßt ihre Kinder*. Köln: Kiepenheuer & Witsch, 1955.

Lyttelton, Adrian. *The Seizure of Power: Fascism in Italy, 1919–1929*, third edition. London: Routledge, 2004.

Majewska, Ewa. *Feminist Antifascism: Counterpublics of the Common*. London: Verso, 2012.

"Manifesto da Frente Unica Anti-Fascista ao Povo do Brasil." *Homem Livre*. July 17, 1933, p. 6.

Melati, Sintha [Umi Sardjono]. "In the Service of the Underground: The Struggle Against the Japanese in Java." In *Local Opposition and Underground Resistance to the Japanese in Java, 1942–1945*, ed. Anton Lucas. Melbourne: Centre of Southeast Asian Studies, Monash University, 1986.

"Mensaje de Beatriz Allende al pueblo chileno." *Granma*. Sept. 11, 1974, p. 2.

"O Movimento Anarco-Punk e a luta antifascista no Brasil." In *Antifa: Modo de usar*, ed. Acácio Augusto. Rio de Janeiro: Hedra, 2020.

Narayan, Jayaprakash. "To All Fighters for Freedom." In *Jayaprakash Narayan: Essential Writings (1929–1979)*, ed. Bimal Prasad. Delhi: Konark, 2002.

"Never Again!" *Searchlight: The Anti-Fascist Monthly* 126 (Dec. 1985): 2.

Newton, Ronald C. "*Ducini, Prominenti, Antifascisti*: Italian Fascism and the Italo-Argentine Collectivity, 1922–1945." *Americas* 51, no. 1 (July 1994): 41–66.

"Note alla seduta." *Avanti!* Nov. 24, 1918, p. 1.

"Notizie di Milano." *Avanti!* Dec. 11, 1916, p. 3.

Padmore, George. *How Britain Rules Africa*. 1936; New York: Negro University Press, 1969.

Patterson, William L., editor. *We Charge Genocide: The Historic Petition to the United Nations for Relief from a Crime of the United States Government against the Negro People*. New York: Civil Rights Congress, 1951.

Paxton, Robert O. "The Five Stages of Fascism." *Journal of Modern History* 70, no. 1 (Mar. 1998): 1–23.

Paxton, Robert O. *The Anatomy of Fascism*. New York: Knopf, 2004.

Poulantzas, Nicos. *Fascisme et dictature: la IIIe Internationale face au fascism*. Paris: Maspéro, 1970.

Pritchard, Gareth. *Niemandsland: A History of Unoccupied Germany, 1944–1945*. Cambridge: Cambridge University Press, 2012.

"Prosigue desarrollandose en todo el mundo la jornada internacional de solidaridad con la lucha del pueblo chileno contra el fascismo." *Granma*. Sept. 10, 1974, p. 1.

Pugliese, Stanislao G., editor. *Fascism, Anti-Fascism, and the Resistance in Italy: 1919 to the Present*. Lanham, MD: Rowman & Littlefield, 2004.

Punk, Helmostro [Mauri Kurcbard]. "Guerra civil punkoide." *Fin de siglo* (Oct. 1987): 41.

Rebelde (Aug. 28, 1971).

Rein, Raanan. "The Meites Sisters and the Spanish Civil War: Women's Support for Republican Spain from Within and Without." *Journal of Modern Jewish Studies* 22, no. 4 (2023): 503–521.

Report of an Amnesty International Mission to The Republic of the Philippines, 22 November–5 December 1975. Wembley: Amnesty International Publications, 1976.

"Riot in Philadelphia." *New York Times*. July 4, 1924, p. 6.

Rivanera Carlés, Federico. *El judaísmo y la semana trágica: La verdadera historia de los sucesos de enero de 1919*. Buenos Aires: Instituto de Investigaciones sobre la Cuestión Judía, 1986.

Rivanera Carlès, Federico. "¿Un estado judío en Argentina?" *Ataque*. Oct. 13, 1986, p. 1.

Rivanera Carlés, Federico. *Los judíos son nuestros enemigos!* Buenos Aires: Instituto de Investigaciones sobre la Cuestión Judía, 1987.

Robeson, Paul. "An Important Message from Paul Robeson." *Spotlight on Africa* 11, no. 2 (Feb. 25, 1952): 1.

Rodríguez, Gonzalo, and Tomás Catavi. "Bolivia: Una lección para la izquierda." *Punto Final: Documentos* (supplement). Sept. 14, 1971, pp. 1–13.

Rosenhaft, Eve. *Beating the Fascists? The German Communists and Political Violence, 1929–1933*. Cambridge: Cambridge University Press, 1983.

Rostow, W. W. *The Stages of Economic Growth: A Non-Communist Manifesto*. Cambridge: Cambridge University Press, 1960.

Salgado, Plínio. "Como eu vi a Itália." *Hierarchia* (Mar. 1932): 202–205.

Scalice, Joseph. *The Drama of Dictatorship: Martial Law and the Communist Parties of the Philippines*. Ithaca: Southeast Asia Program Publications, 2023.

Scalp, 1984–1992: Comme un indien métropolitain: Aux origins du movement antifasciste radical. Paris: No Pasaran, 2005.

Sechaba (Jan. 1967).

Selth, Andrew, "Race and Resistance in Burma, 1942–1945." *Modern Asian Studies* 20, no. 3 (1986): 483–507.

"Settlers Criticise Government." *Times of India*. Oct. 8, 1935, p. 5.

Shaw, Vivian. "Strategies of Ambivalence: Cultures of Liberal Antifa in Japan." *Radical History Review*, no. 138 (Oct. 2020): 145–170.

Shibuichi, Daiki. "The Struggle Against Hate Groups in Japan: The Invisible Civil Society, Leftist Elites and Anti-Racism Groups." *Social Science Japan Journal* 19, no. 1 (Winter 2016): 71–83.

Smith, Martin. *Burma: Insurgency and the Politics of Ethnicity*. London: Zed, 1991.

Snowden, Frank M. *Violence and Great Estates in the South of Italy: Apulia, 1900–1922*. Cambridge: Cambridge University Press, 1986.

Sonabend, Daniel. *We Fight Fascists: The 43 Group and Their Forgotten Battle for Post-war Britain*. London: Verso, 2019.

South Africa – Uncensored. Council on African Affairs, 1951. 21 min. https://nmaahc.si.edu/object/nmaahc_2012.79.1.5.1a#.

"South Africans at Nation-wide April 6 Protest Rallies Pledge All-out Campaign of Defiance against Unjust Laws." *Spotlight on Africa* 11, no. 5 (Apr. 14, 1952): 2.

Spotlight on Africa 11, no. 5 (Apr. 14, 1952).

Stocker, Paul. *Lost Imperium: Far Right Visions of the British Empire, c. 1920–1980*. Abingdon: Routledge, 2021.

"Sühne für die Altonaer Erwerbslosen-krawalle." *Altonaer Nachrichten*. Mar. 28, 1930, p. 5.

"Support the South African People's Campaign Against Fascist Enslavement." *Spotlight on Africa* 11, no. 2 (Feb. 25, 1952): 2.

Taylor, Robert H. "Burma in the Anti-Fascist War." In *Southeast Asia under Japanese Occupation*, ed. Alfred W. McCoy. New Haven: Yale University Southeast Asia Studies, 1980.

Taylor, Robert H. *Marxism and Resistance in Burma, 1942–1945: Thein Pe Myint's Wartime Traveler*. Athens: Ohio University Press, 1984.

Teba, Monk. "Cabrini Green Housing Projects … the Same as the Warsaw Ghetto of Poland in 1942." *Black Panther*. Dec. 14, 1970, p. 5.

"To All Diliman Communards." *Bandilang Pula*. Feb. 12, 1971, p. B.

Torrado, Sergio Yanes, Carlos Marín Suárez, and María Cantabrana Carassou. *Papeles de plomo: Los voluntarios uruguayos en la Guerra Civil Española*. Montevideo: Banda Oriental, 2017.

Traverso, Enzo. *Left-Wing Melancholia: Marxism, History, and Memory.* New York: Columbia University Press, 2016.

Tresca, Carlo. "Fascismo e Fascisti." *Martello.* Mar. 12, 1921, p. 1.

Tsou, Hwei-Ru, and Len Tsou. *Los brigadistas chinos en la guerra civil: La llamada de España (1936–1939)*, trans. Laureano Ramírez Bellerín. Madrid: Catarata, 2013.

Tun Thwin. *The Impact of Political Thought on Burma's Struggle for Independence (1930–1948).* Ann Arbor: Center for South and Southeast Asian Studies, 1989.

"L'ultima speculazione." *Avanti!* May 26, 1922, p. 1.

Vecchione, Marc-Aurèle, director. *Antifa: Chasseurs de skins.* Résistance Films, 2008. 1 hr., 5 min. www.youtube.com/watch?v=soIUEkICiVU.

Verbitsky, Horacio. "Reflexiones para evitar otra derrota." *Fin de siglo* (Aug. 1987): 39.

Vergnon, Gilles. *L'antifascisme en France: De Mussolini à Le Pen.* Rennes: Presses universitaires de Rennes, 2009.

Vysotsky, Stanislav. *American Antifa: The Tactics, Culture, and Practice of Militant Antifascism.* Abingdon: Routledge, 2021.

Wieviorka, Olivier. *The Resistance in Western Europe, 1940–1945*, trans. Jane Marie Todd. New York: Columbia University Press, 2019.

Wilder, Gary. *Concrete Utopianism: The Politics of Temporality and Solidarity.* New York: Fordham University Press, 2022.

Wolf, Simon. "Genocide: The Crime That Is No Longer Nameless." *Unity: A Magazine of Jewish Affairs* 2, no. 3 (Sept. 1949): 13–14.

Zuckerman, Yitzhak ("Antek"). *A Surplus of Memory: Chronicle of the Warsaw Ghetto Uprising*, trans. Barbara Harshav. Berkeley: University of California Press, 1993.

Cambridge Elements

The History and Politics of Fascism

Series Editors
Federico Finchelstein
The New School for Social Research

Federico Finchelstein is Professor of History at the New School for Social Research and Eugene Lang College in New York City. He is an expert on fascism, populism, and dictatorship. His previous books include *From Fascism to Populism in History* and *A Brief History of Fascist Lies*.

António Costa Pinto
University of Lisbon

António Costa Pinto is a Research Professor at the Institute of Social Sciences, University of Lisbon. He is a specialist in fascism, authoritarian politics, and political elites. He is the author and editor of multiple books on fascism, including (with Federico Finchelstein) *Authoritarianism and Corporatism in Europe and Latin America*.

Advisory Board
Giulia Albanese, *University of Padova*
Mabel Berezin, *Cornell University*
Maggie Clinton, *Middlebury College*
Sandra McGee Deutsch, *University of Texas, El Paso*
Aristotle Kallis, *Keele University*
Sven Reichardt, *University of Konstanz*
Angelo Ventrone, *University of Macerata*

About the Series
Cambridge Elements in the History and Politics of Fascism is a series that provides a platform for cutting-edge comparative research in the field of fascism studies. With a broad theoretical, empirical, geographic, and temporal scope, it will cover all regions of the world, and most importantly, search for new and innovative perspectives.

Cambridge Elements

The History and Politics of Fascism

Elements in the Series

Populism and Fascism
Carlos de la Torre

The Rise of Mass Parties, Liberal Italy, and the Fascist Dawn (1919–1924)
Goffredo Adinolfi

Neo-Fascism and the Far Right in Brazil
Odilon Caldeira Neto

Intellectual Post-fascism?: The Conservative Revolution, Traditionalism and the Challenge to Liberal Democracy
Alberto Spektorowski

The Fascist Zenith: War and Dictatorship under Axis Rule
António Costa Pinto

The Five Ages of Antifascism
Joseph Fronczak

A full series listing is available at: www.cambridge.org/CEHF

For EU product safety concerns, contact us at Calle de José Abascal, 56–1°, 28003 Madrid, Spain or eugpsr@cambridge.org.

www.ingramcontent.com/pod-product-compliance
Lightning Source LLC
LaVergne TN
LVHW011849060526
838200LV00054B/4257